D1565030

BLACK NOVELISTS

AND THE

SOUTHERN

LITERARY TRADITION

BLACK NOVELISTS

AND THE

SOUTHERN

LITERARY   TRADITION

Ladell Payne

The University of Georgia Press / Athens

Copyright © 1981 by the University of Georgia Press, Athens 30602
ALL RIGHTS RESERVED
Second printing 1982

Set in VIP Caledonia
Printed in the United States of America
Design by Design for Publishing

Library of Congress Cataloging in Publication Data

Payne, Ladell.
    Black novelists and the Southern literary tradition.

    Includes index.
    1. American literature—Afro-American authors—His-
tory and criticism.   2. American literature—20th century—History and criticism.   I. Title.
PS153.N5P39   813'.009'896073   80-21747
                ISBN 0-8203-0536-7

For my relatives and ancestors—

Paynes and McBrayers and Taylors

Clyde and Gerusia

Lisa and Jennifer

and especially for Jean,

who has given so much

Contents

I/3
Relatives and Ancestors

II/9
Trunk and Branch: *Charles Waddell Chesnutt, 1858–1932*

III/26
Themes and Cadences: *James Weldon Johnson, 1871–1938*

IV/38
Song of the South: *Jean Toomer, 1894–1967*

V/54
A Clear Case: *Richard Wright, 1908–1960*

VI/80
The Shadow of the Past: *Ralph Ellison, 1914–*

VII/99
Products of the Southern Condition

103
Notes

111
Index

Acknowledgments

This book could not have been written without the support of a National Endowment for the Humanities Fellowship which allowed me the free time essential for extensive reading and preliminary writing. I am grateful to the National Endowment not only for the specific benefits of this grant to me, but also for the larger effects that N E H grants of all kinds are having on the humanities nationally.

I owe a debt of thanks to Claremont Men's College for allowing me a leave of absence to accept the N E H Fellowship and for awarding me a faculty grant to support additional summer research.

I am grateful to the editors of the following journals for their permission to reprint materials that have appeared earlier in somewhat different form: *Americana-Austriaca* for "Trunk and Branch: Charles Waddell Chesnutt, 1858–1932," and *The Southern Literary Journal* for "Themes and Cadences: James Weldon Johnson as Black Southern Novelist."

I owe personal debts to some of my past and present colleagues at the Claremont Black Studies Center, many of whom, while disagreeing with my particular approach to black literature, were unfailingly helpful and generous. Agnes Jackson, who teaches a seminar on Faulkner and Wright for Pitzer College and has served as acting director of the B.S.C., introduced me to the black academic community. Alonzo Smith was most helpful in guiding my reading in black history and in suggesting bibliographical materials. Stanley Crouch generously shared with me his impressions from an interview with Ralph Ellison and his insights into what we both see as shared elements of black and white southern culture.

I am profoundly grateful to Susan Stewart, Augusta Colonna, Miriam Clark, and, most especially, Mary Ellen Isaac for struggling heroically with my illegible handwriting and C M C's antiquated dictating equipment as they prepared the various drafts of my text while managing the ongoing work of the Literature Department. Katherine Davis Davis and Andrea Faeder of Randolph-Macon College performed a similar service in preparing the final revision. I am grateful also to Dr. Douglas W. Cooper, Reference Librarian at Randolph-Macon's Walter Hines Page Library, who generously helped with bibliographical references, and to Mrs. Hilde Robinson, whose careful copyediting and critical comments were invaluable.

My greatest personal debt is to Robert H. Fossum, Josephine Olp Weeks Professor of Literature at C M C, who served as critic, counselor, and friend throughout the project. To paraphrase one of Miss Reba's associates, thanks, Bob, for "cheering for me."

LADELL PAYNE

Randolph-Macon College
Claremont Men's College

BLACK NOVELISTS

AND THE

SOUTHERN

LITERARY TRADITION

I

Relatives and Ancestors

While one can do nothing about choosing one's relatives, one can, as artist, choose one's "ancestors." Wright was, in this sense, a "relative"; Hemingway. . . . and Malraux and Dostoevsky and Faulkner, were "ancestors."

—Ralph Ellison,
"The World and the Jug"

Ralph Ellison made his remarks about literary relatives and ancestors in 1964 in his well-known response to Irving Howe's 1963 essay, "Black Boys and Native Sons." At issue was Howe's assertion that neither Ellison nor James Baldwin was a true "native son" in the tradition of their literary father Richard Wright because both rejected Wright's artistic methods and held visions of American life that deviated from Wright's clenched militancy. The thrust of Ellison's response is that a serious writer is concerned with art, not social propaganda. His obligation, therefore, is to master the techniques of his craft so that he can best present his individual vision of human experience. Ellison denies that Richard Wright is the literary father of all contemporary black writers, and says that "the notion of an intellectual or artistic succession based upon color or racial background is no less absurd than one based upon a common religious background." Ellison, of course, is not denying the value of understanding the social or cultural forces that form the milieu out of which any artist creates. Certainly he is not ignoring the importance of his own identity as a twentieth-century American Negro reared in Oklahoma and educated at Tuskegee, Alabama. He insists, however, upon the complexity of this background, the interrelatedness of black and white American culture, and the fallaciousness of any overly simple categorizing.

A part of the complexity of the black writer's experience springs from his roots in the American South. The South was his home from the time of Jamestown until the time of Appomattox, indeed until the time of the great migrations North impelled by World Wars I and II. Most northern Negroes even today can be no more than two or three generations removed from the South. Yet, at least as far as literary criticism is concerned, little consideration has been given to the recognizably southern qualities which inform much of what is now called black literature. Nor has attention been paid to the possibility of there being any specific literary relationship between the black authors who grew up or were largely educated in the South and the white authors from the same region. This is especially surprising when one considers the plethora of recent critical studies devoted both to southern and black writers, studies that have tended to be as segregated as the two races.[1]

Even those who do mention the black southern writers tend to consider them to be outside the great tradition. John M. Bradbury's comment is indicative: "Southern-born Negroes have not as yet produced a Renaissance of their own, though a handful have contributed to the general American awakening of Negro literary talent. . . . Judged by the standards of Southern white-authored fiction, the Negro novels appear undistinguished in artistry and thin in substance."[2] Frederick J. Hoffman argues on artistic grounds that a black southern writer is primarily a black writer: "Such a phenomenon as the Negro novel has a southern point of reference, surely, but the South becomes mainly a sociological, a psychological, and a moral reference point in this case. There is a world of difference between Faulkner's or Miss Welty's or Mrs. McCullers' view of the Negro, and the Negro's view of himself (as in the case of Richard Wright's *Black Boy* and the first part of Ralph Ellison's *Invisible Man*); it is as though they were treating of vastly different kinds of being. This is because the Negro novelist is largely a *displaced* Southerner."[3] Hoffman's observation is interesting both for what is said and for what is implied. Obviously, the southern Negro writer's perception of a black man's experience differs from that of the southern white writer. Hoffman implies, however, that there is a transcending difference in kind. Does Wright's Bigger Thomas really have more in common with Ellison's "I" than either has with Faulkner's Joe Christmas? Do Jean Toomer's poetic descriptions of the Georgia people and land really reflect the impulses of the Harlem school more than they do those of an entire raft of failed southern poets? Is not the white southern writer also, as Louis D. Rubin, Jr., has noted, in a sense a displaced southerner?[4] The answers to these and other similar questions do not seem as self-evident to me as Hoffman would suggest.

The critics who have dealt with black literature also have been almost exclusively concerned with the qualities that are common to Negro writers *qua* Negroes. Houston A. Baker, Jr., states the extreme position:

Black America can justifiably say that it possesses a true culture—a *whole* way of life that includes its own standards of moral and aesthetic achievement. . . . One index of the distinctiveness of black American culture is the extent to which it repudiates the culture theorizing of the white Western world. . . . Thus, repudiation . . . is one of the most important factors in setting black American literature apart from white American literature. . . . Call it black, Afro-American, Negro, the fact remains that there is a fundamental, qualitative difference between [black] and white American culture. Plato, E. M. Forster, Baudelaire, and many others at the heart of what white America calls culture have only the remotest connection with black American culture.[5]

More typical, and in my judgment more balanced, is the attitude of Robert A. Bone: "The Negro novel, like Negro life in America, is at once alike and different from the novels of white Americans. . . . The American Negro . . . has not one but two cultures to interpret. . . . He must be conversant with Western culture as a whole, and especially with the traditions of English literature of which he is a part, and at the same time be prepared to affirm a Negro quality in his experience, exploiting his Negro heritage as a legitimate contribution to the larger culture."[6]

Some few critics of the two literatures, while pursuing their separate interests, have moved within a step or two of the questions which I wish to consider in this study. Edward Margolies and Saunders Redding both agree, for example, with Arna Bontemps's judgment that Richard Wright "remained not only an American but a Southerner. . . . His deepest roots were in the folk culture of the bottom—not *deep* but *bottom*—South."[7] Similarly, Louis D. Rubin, Jr., in the preface to his most thoroughgoing exploration of the white writer's relationship to the southern community, suggests that black writers from the South are indeed southerners even though outside the limits of his study. "Finally I have said absolutely nothing about an increasingly important aspect of the southern literary scene, the black southern writer. . . . For the black southern writer, whether he be Charles Chesnutt or James Weldon Johnson or Jean Toomer or Richard Wright or Ralph Ellison, obviously has been involved in a relationship to southern society and southern attitudes that is very different from that of the white southern author, so that my generalizations and suppositions about the community relationship would require a whole new kind of approach and examination."[8]

That the cultural experiences of the southern black and white writers in this country differ to greater and lesser degrees is a truth universally acknowledged. Nothing I will say in the following essays is intended to deny or belittle these differences. But it seems to me that there is enough prima facie evidence to justify an exploration of the elements which unite such writers as southerners. Southern writers, black and white, utilize common sources and illustrate common values. Both literatures clearly draw upon a folk culture, grow out of evangelical Protestantism, and rely on oral narrative devices; both literatures characteristically emphasize a sense of locus, stress the importance of family, are concerned about the relationship between man and history, and dwell on an individual's search for identity at a time of social chaos; finally, at their best, both literatures deal honestly with black-white relationships.

The novel is clearly the dominant form employed by southern writers, black or white. It would be difficult at best to argue for a southern literary renascence without the works of Twain, Warren, Faulkner, Cabell, Glasgow, Wolfe, Welty, Caldwell, O'Connor, McCullers, and Styron. Novelists have also dominated southern black

letters. George Wylie Henderson, Ernest Gaines, Edward Waters
Turpin, William Attaway, Margaret Walker, Zora Neale Hurston,
Arna Bontemps, and Ishmael Reed are names which quickly come
to mind as black southern novelists of distinction. Indeed, each of
these latter writers might well have been the subject of a study such
as this one. My intention, however, is to write a representative
rather than a comprehensive study. I will focus my attention, therefore, on the relationships which exist between a few important
black southern novelists—Charles Waddell Chesnutt, James Weldon Johnson, Jean Toomer, Richard Wright, and Ralph Ellison—
and their white colleagues. My reason for selecting these authors is
self-evident; their lives and works are important in themselves and
they span the time from Reconstruction to the present. Richard
Wright and Ralph Ellison are generally recognized as writers of national prominence. Charles Waddell Chesnutt, described as "the
best writer of prose fiction the race had produced" until the early
twentieth century,[9] is the first black southern novelist to attract
general recognition. James Weldon Johnson, "the only true artist
among the early Negro novelists,"[10] and Jean Toomer, who "has
written of the South with so much sense of pain and beauty inextricably linked,"[11] were writing before either Faulkner or Richard
Wright.

Finally, a few brief words about definitions. It seems to me that
the terms *Southern* and *Negro*, like the term *novel*, are subject to
broad, general, but not very precise definition. I find myself react-
ing to all of these terms very much as did the Supreme Court Justice who said that although he could not define pornography, he
thought he knew it when he saw it. We all remember the intellectual energy and ingenuity spent half a century ago defining when,
exactly, a short story becomes a novella and a novella becomes a
novel; why Richardson is the first novelist rather than Defoe; and
why *Gulliver's Travels* is or is not a novel. This work was most helpful in explaining Henry James, but really did little to prepare us for
the mutations imposed upon traditional fiction in our time. More
recently, John M. Bradbury has defined a southern writer as "one
who was born and lived his formative years" in the region which
includes Kentucky, Maryland, east Arkansas, east Texas, the Shen-
andoah Valley of West Virginia, and the rest of the Confederate

states except for that portion of Florida currently controlled by
Yankees.[12] Such a definition, like a definition of the novel, is gener-
ally helpful. But it excludes Samuel Clemens, even though his was a
slave-owning family, Missouri was a slave state, and the life of a
Mississippi riverboat pilot had nothing culturally to do with west
Texas or Ozark, Arkansas. Above all, however, Clemens's *Huckleberry Finn* is, by any definition I can accept, a southern novel.[13]
Much more helpful, it seems to me, are studies such as those by
Frederick J. Hoffman, C. Hugh Holman, and Louis D. Rubin[14]
which, like E. M. Forster's great study of the novel, deal with characteristic aspects rather than with page numbers or exact geograph-
ical borders. Since I am dealing with a limited number of authors
and works, I will give my reasons for considering Ellison a southerner, Toomer a black, and *Cane* a novel as I discuss the specific
aspects these writers and their works share with their white confreres, their southern relatives and ancestors.

II

Trunk and Branch
Charles Waddell Chesnutt, 1858–1932

Measured in psychological, sociological and raw cultural terms, the distinction and the differences
between writing by American Negroes and other Americans are justified. But for all that, it is only the
distinction between trunk and branch. The writing of
Negroes is fed by the same roots sunk in the same cultural soil as writing by white Americans.
— Saunders Redding,
"The Negro Writer and American Literature"

Charles Waddell Chesnutt, de-
scribed as "the best writer of prose fiction the race had produced"
until the early twentieth century,[1] is the first black southern novelist to gain prominence. Born on 20 June 1858 in Cleveland, Ohio,[2]
Charles Waddell Chesnutt was descended from North Carolina free
Negroes. In 1856 Ann Marie and Chloe Sampson, Chesnutt's
mother and grandmother to be, moved by wagon train from Fayetteville, North Carolina, to Cleveland. The following year Ann
Marie married Andrew Jackson Chesnutt, a participant in the same
exodus. Charles Waddell was born a year later, five years before
emancipation. In 1866 the family returned to Reconstruction-era
North Carolina, where Charles lived until the summer of 1883,
when he turned twenty-five. He received his formal education at
the Howard School of Fayetteville. At fourteen, he became a part-
time teacher at the school and began a lifelong habit of broad
reading and study. Through a combination of hired tutors and self-

9

instruction, Chesnutt learned Latin, Greek, French, German, and shorthand. He could also play the piano and organ. Caucasian in appearance,[3] young Chesnutt either deliberately "passed" or was mistaken for white on more than one occasion. His journal for April 1879 reveals a Horatio Alger–like dream of going North and getting a job on the staff of some good newspaper. Then, in his words, he would "work, work, work! . . . trust in God and work."

For three years Charles assisted at a school in Charlotte, North Carolina, during the regular term and taught at various Carolina rural schools in the summer. At eighteen he became principal of a public school in Charlotte; at nineteen he was appointed to the faculty of the New State Colored Normal School established in Fayetteville to train Negro teachers. Before he was twenty, Charles married fellow-teacher Susan Perry. In 1880 the twenty-two-year-old Chesnutt became principal of the Normal School. He was also serving the Methodist church as organist, choir master, and superintendent of the Sunday school. During this time Chesnutt worked to perfect his stenographic skills so that he would be able to go North. In 1883 he resigned the principalship of the most important Negro school in North Carolina and moved first to New York, as a reporter for Dow Jones and Company, then to Cleveland as an accountant with the Nickel Plate Railroad. Within a year he had been transferred to the railroad's legal department, where he studied law while working as a stenographer. In his spare time he wrote essays, poems, short stories, and sketches. By the time he was twenty-nine, a number of his pieces had been published locally and the *Atlantic Monthly* had accepted the "Goophered Grapevine," the first of his conjure stories. The same year he also passed the Ohio Bar examination with distinction.

Continuing more or less simultaneously the careers of courtroom stenographer, lawyer, and fiction writer, Chesnutt published three books in 1899: *The Conjure Woman, The Wife of His Youth and Other Stories of the Color Line*, and a biography of Frederick Douglass. Like the "Goophered Grapevine," which was included, the conjure stories were written in dialect and drew upon the Negro witchcraft folklore of his native North Carolina. In these tales Chesnutt reverses a basic convention of the form popularized by the Uncle Remus stories of Joel Chandler Harris. Unlike Uncle Remus, who, although sympathetically treated, is a source of amusement for the more sophisticated white reader, Chesnutt's Uncle Julius has the last laugh himself because he has played his role of foolish ignorance successfully to deceive the apparently more sophisticated white man.[4] Most of the colorline stories deal with the problems of a variety of "tragic mulattoes," Afro-Americans so white in appearance that classifying them as blacks is patently irrational.[5] After the turn of the century, Chesnutt published three novels: *The House behind the Cedars* (1900), *The Marrow of Tradition* (1901), and *The Colonel's Dream* (1905). The first two also focus on Afro-Americans of mixed blood; all three are concerned with post–Civil War racial relationships in the South.

Chesnutt's critical reception initially was very favorable. Fellow southerners Walter Hines Page, who edited the *Atlantic Monthly*, and George W. Cable, then at the height of his fame, liked the conjure stories. So did William Dean Howells, who wrote an essay praising Chesnutt rather extravagantly as a conscious artist who "seems to know quite as well what he wants to do in a given case as Maupassant, or Tourguénief, or Mr. James . . . and has done it with an art of kindred quiet and force."[6] But generally both public and critical response to Chesnutt's novels was less enthusiastic. Perceived by some to be militantly bitter, these novels did not sell. Distressed by the economic returns and saddened by his fiction's failure to improve racial relations in this country, Chesnutt stopped writing. Then, in 1927, near seventy years of age, he wrote *The Quarry*, a novel his publisher would not accept. Although disappointed, Chesnutt had been to some degree compensated. On 8 June 1928 he received a telegram, appropriately enough from James Weldon Johnson, informing him of his selection by the NAACP to receive the fourteenth annual Spingarn Medal for his "pioneer work as a literary artist depicting the life and struggles of Americans of Negro descent." And to his delight, a new edition of *The Conjure Woman* was published in 1929. He died in 1932, honored as a man, respected as a minor writer.

Three years before he left North Carolina, seven years before the "Goophered Grapevine" appeared in the *Atlantic Monthly*, a decade before his first novel, Charles Waddell Chesnutt wrote in his journal:

May 29, 1880
I think I must write a book. . . . Fifteen years of life in the South, in
one of the most eventful eras of its history, among a people whose
life is rich in the elements of romance, under conditions calculated
to stir one's soul to the very depths—I think there is here a fund of
experience, a supply of material, which a skillful pen could work up
with tremendous effect. Besides, if I do write, I shall write for a
purpose, a high, holy purpose, and this will inspire me to greater
effort. The object of my writings would be not so much the elevation of the colored people as the elevation of the whites—for I consider the unjust spirit of caste which is so insidious as to pervade a
whole nation, and so powerful as to subject a whole race and all connected with it to scorn and social ostracism—I consider this a barri-
er to the moral progress of the American people.[7]

This statement could well have been Chesnutt's literary manifesto.
Certainly he uses southern Negro folk materials from the antebellum plantation South for his conjure stories. Like his fellow
North Carolinian, Thomas Wolfe, Chesnutt used the town where he
grew up as the thinly disguised location for his fiction.[8] But it is in
his novels that Chesnutt deals most explicitly and most characteristically with the evils of caste. And it is two of his novels that I wish
to examine in some detail to suggest the extent to which Chesnutt is
not only a black man from the South who wrote novels, but also a
southern novelist. These are *The House behind the Cedars*, his first
and most popular novel, and *The Marrow of Tradition*, his most
forthright presentation of the racial problem in the South and the
book which finally cost him his readership.[9]
    Set in "Patesville" (Fayetteville), North Carolina, *The House be-
hind the Cedars* tells the story of John and Rena Walden, children
of "a free colored woman" named "Molly Walden—her rightful
name, for her parents were free-born and legally married."[10] Like
Faulkner's Sam Fathers, Molly is a mixture of black, white, and Indian strains. Years before the Civil War, she becomes the mistress
of a distinguished gentleman who gives her a small house behind a
cedar hedge, a store of gold pieces, and the promise of future provision in a will "which never came to light." A few years before the
Civil War, young John Walden, the Caucasian-featured son of this
union, decides that he will "pass." He is taken in as office boy by
Judge Archibald Straight, who allows him to read law secretly out of

friendship for John's dead father. At eighteen John leaves Molly and his seven-year-old sister and goes off to seek his fortune. As the novel opens, John has been away ten years and is returning incognito to Patesville. He is now John Warwick, a South Carolina gentleman. Escaping service in the Confederate Army in some vague way, made wealthy by a wife he married during the social upheaval after the war, he has established a genteel law practice in Clarence (Charleston), South Carolina. John's wife has recently died and he is left with an infant son. He returns to Patesville to persuade the now seventeen-year-old Rena to join him in South Carolina. She agrees, and after a brief stint at a finishing school, appears in Clarence as Rowena Warwick. There she is quickly wooed by and betrothed to George Tryon, a North Carolina gentleman. Before they can be married, however, Rena returns to Patesville to care for her sick mother. By coincidence, Tryon also appears in Patesville and discovers Rena's true identity. Although Tryon does not expose the Warwick deception, he cancels the wedding. Rena decides to enter the nineteenth-century North Carolina equivalent of a nunnery. She renounces the vanity of the white world and devotes herself as a teacher to improving the Negro race. Burying herself in a small rural school, which, unknown to her, is near the Tryon family estate, Rena finds herself pursued on the one hand by George Tryon and on the other by a lecherous mulatto school superintendent. Fleeing them both, Rena is overcome by nervous exhaustion and dies.

The most important thematic element that Chesnutt's first novel shares with many other southern novels, both earlier and later, is the protagonist's movement from innocence to knowledge and its effect upon the character's sense of identity. Of course, a protagonist's loss of innocence and concomitant discovery of himself is a novelistic concern which goes back at least as far as *Joseph Andrews* in the English tradition. In our national fiction, we have a multitude of American Adams seeking to regain the Garden of Eden. The southern writer seems almost unable to write without creating protagonists, usually in their youth, who first lose their innocence and then, characteristically, find themselves. Twain's Huck Finn; Faulkner's Ike McCaslin, Lucius Priest, Thomas Sutpen, and Chick Mallison; Capote's Joel Knox; Wolfe's Eugene Gant and George

Webber; McCullers's Mick Kelley; Warren's Willie Stark; Styron's Nat Turner—the list seems almost endless. A recent reviewer states the case: "Perhaps it has something to do with the old Southern blend of agrarian idealism and the 18th century romance with the noble savage. Or maybe it is just all that ambling through the tall grass. In any case, Southern writers have had a particular weakness for seeing a beauty and naked truth through the eye of the innocent."[11]

Of course, the nature of a protagonist's innocence and the terms of the identity he achieves vary. The innocence lost by Thomas Sutpen when he decides to define himself as a slave-owning gentleman because he learns that he is considered white trash is not the same as either the innocence of Eugene Gant looking for a lost lane back to his cosmic self or that of almost any of Flannery O'Connor's tortured figures fighting to escape their spiritual identity in the eyes of God.

To Chesnutt, as to almost all black writers northern or southern, achieving personal identity is inextricably interwoven with racial caste. For John Walden to have an identity in *The House behind the Cedars*, he (like Thomas Sutpen) must become a southern white gentleman. And like Sutpen, Walden gets his idea of what a white gentleman must be indirectly. For although Walden's father did not give him a gentleman's family name, he did (like David Copperfield's father) leave him a gentlemanly library: "Fielding's complete works, in fine print, set in double columns; a set of Bulwer's novels; a collection of everything that Walter Scott—the literary idol of the South—had ever written," in addition to the Bible, Shakespeare, Milton, and Bunyan (pp. 145–46). It is through his reading that John loses his innocence and gains knowledge. When Willie Stark learns of evil, Warren baptizes him in liquor. When Mr. Head ("The Artificial Nigger") discovers his pride, O'Connor says that he also recognized his share in the guilt of original sin. Chesnutt follows a similar impulse and describes Walden's transformation in biblical terms. "When he had read all the books—indeed, long before he had read all of them—he too had tasted of the fruit of the Tree of Knowledge: contentment took its flight, and happiness lay far beyond the sphere where he was born. The blood of his white fathers, the heirs of the ages, cried out for its own, and after the

manner of that blood set about getting the object of its desire"
(p. 147).

Without name or estate, young Walden turns to the law as a profession which will provide him with upward mobility in the antebellum South. When he approaches Judge Straight and tells him
that he wants to become a lawyer, the old judge—who, as his name
suggests, represents the aristocratic South at its best—is (like Walden himself) much more concerned with John's race than with his
illegitimate birth. Their confrontation defines both what Walden is
and must remain as a Negro and why becoming a white gentleman
is his only means of attaining an acceptable identity as a man.

"You are aware, of course, that you are a Negro?"
"I am white," replied the lad, turning back his sleeve and holding
out his arm, "and I am free, as all my people were before me."
". . . You are black," he said, "and you are not free. You cannot
travel without your papers; you cannot secure accommodations at
an inn; you could not vote, if you were of age; you cannot be out
after nine o'clock without a permit. If a white man struck you, you
could not return the blow, and you could not testify against him in a
court of justice. You are black, my lad, and you are not free."
(p. 152)

Judge Straight violates the customs of his caste and allows John to
use his library so long as no one else knows about it. He further
advises John to go to South Carolina, because his race, if ques-
tioned, could be decided legally "by reputation, by reception into
society, and by [the] exercise of the privileges of the white man, as
well as by admixture of blood" (p. 154). John follows Straight's advice and, despite his sister's disappointment and subsequent death,
is at the novel's end living as a wealthy white South Carolina lawyer-
gentleman in "the land of his father where, he conceived, he had an
inalienable birth right" (p. 21).

Unlike her brother, Rena Walden suffers from no problems of
knowing who she is, at least initially. A dutiful daughter, she accepts
her life with her mother in the house behind the cedars, vaguely
hoping in some indefinite way that she will be able to teach, now
that the Yankees have started schools for both poor whites and
blacks. When John offers her the chance to join him in South Carolina, however, and their mother acquiesces, she readily accepts.

The life which Rena and John leave, though socially repressed, is humanly rich. Like Dickens's Pip, they leave the reality of loving friends and family and enter an artificial society. Chesnutt suggests early in the novel that they are entering a fantasy world when black John Walden becomes white John Warwick, an identity borrowed not from the world of fact but from the world of romantic fiction. "From Bulwer's novel, he had read the story of Warwick the King-maker, and upon leaving home had chosen it for his own. He was a new man, but he had the blood of an old race, and he would select for his own one of its worthy names" (p. 27). Similarly, Rena Walden becomes Rowena Warwick, after the heroine of *Ivanhoe*. She makes her entrance into society on the day of the Clarence Social Club's annual tournament. Like Rena's new name, the tournament is bor-rowed directly from Scott's *Ivanhoe* and serves both as an emblem of and an ironic commentary on the white South. Chesnutt tells us with a straight face that during the month preceding the tourna-ment, the local bookseller had sold his entire stock of *Ivanhoe* (some five copies) and had ordered seven copies more. With the "best people" in the grandstand, and the poor whites and Negroes in the bleachers, masquerading knights in colorful costumes of gilded cloth, paper, and cardboard prepare to attack wooden blocks with their swords and pierce iron rings with their wooden lances.[12] It is, as John Warwick says with unconscious irony, "the renaissance of chivalry." But it is not a renaissance of historic chivalry (whatever that was); it is a late nineteenth-century South Carolina adaptation of Scott's early nineteenth-century romanticized fiction. And it is a renaissance, again as John Warwick says, which substitutes card-board costumes for the discomfort of armor, which retains the for-mality of lists and knights and prancing steeds but eliminates the possibility of physical risk. It is, like the worst aspects of southern chivalry, a picturesque but bloodless display. George Tryon, in a per-formance worthy of a gilded Black Knight or cardboard Wilfred of Ivanhoe, wins the tourney and names Rowena Warwick as Queen of Love and Beauty at the post-tourney ball. The entire episode recalls the tournament at Ashby-de-la-Zouche in many ways. Scott's tour-nament was between the conquering Normans and the oppressed but worthy Saxons. It is the Saxon Lady Rowena who is named Queen of Honor and Love by Ivanhoe. In South Carolina, all identify themselves with the Saxons; actually, however, Rowena is more nearly analogous to the Jewess Rebecca. Like Rebecca, she loses both the man she loves and a proper place in society because of her race. In Scott's novel, the wedding of Lady Rowena and Ivanhoe is attended by both highborn Normans and Saxons, thus marking "the marriage of two individuals as a pledge of the future peace and harmony betwixt two races, which, since that period, had been so completely mingled, that the distinction has become wholly invisible" (*Ivanhoe*, chapter 44). Of course no such resolution occurs in nineteenth-century South Carolina, although the eradication of racial distinctions is Chesnutt's aim. The irony he conveys through his chivalric parallels is that despite the influence of Scott upon the old South, white southerners were blind to the applicability of the attack upon racial discrimination implicit in *Ivanhoe*.

John Warwick consistently accepts and defends the values of the South Carolina pseudo-renaissance. He states without conscious irony that the Clarence tourney is superior to the tournaments of the older times. "The spirit of a thing, after all, is what counts; and what is lacking here?" (p. 44). By extension, of course, he is defending his new identity as a white southern gentleman. Never throughout the novel does he question this identity or the values it embodies. Rena, on the other hand, while dazzled by the glamour of her new role as Queen of Love and Beauty and sincerely in love with her new knight-errant, never blindly accepts either the reality of white society or her new identity within it. On the evening of the grand ball she still recalls her life in Patesville. "Of the two, the present was more of a dream, the past was the more vivid reality" (p. 55). Her conversation with her brother after the ball suggests the differences in their perceptions. They both recognize that the tournament and ball are fantasy, but they differ as to the nature of reality. John suggests that reality is his life as a southern gentleman. "And now, sister . . . now that the masquerade is over, let us to sleep, and to-morrow take up the serious business of life." Rena, however, says, "It is a dream . . . only a dream. I am Cinderella before the clock has struck" (p. 57). Just as her earlier remarks suggested that her Patesville past was real and the present a dream, so this remark reveals not an awakening to a tomorrow as a South Carolina lady, but a reversion to her former lower state. Similarly, it is not John but Rena who feels that her fiancé must be told about her past. And although she equivocates and does not tell Tryon directly, she does ask him if he would still love her were she the mulatto nurse of John's son. It is Rena who unquestioningly returns to Patesville to care for her sick mother only a few days before the scheduled wedding. And it is Rena who gains the undeniable knowledge that she cannot be white when George Tryon discovers the truth of her racial past. After this catastrophe John Warwick tries to persuade his sister to return with him to South Carolina, because even though Tryon will not now marry Rena, he is a "gentleman" and will be silent. As he has done consistently, John accepts a position based on appearances. Rena prefers her knowledge: "'The law, you said, made us white; but not the law, nor even love can conquer prejudice. . . . I am not sorry that I tried it. It opened my eyes, and I would rather die of knowledge than live in ignorance. . . . I shall never marry any man, and I'll not leave mother again. God is against it; I'll stay with my own people'" (pp. 161–62).

One question Rena must address is, "Who are my people?" The answer is not simple. Rejected as Tryon's wife, she cannot accept him on any other terms. Nor can she ever "again become quite the Rena Walden who had left the house behind the cedars no more than a year and a half before" (p. 191). As Rena Walden, she could have unquestioningly accepted the social values of mulatto society, values which are demonstrated during a mulatto dance party whose borrowed snobbery as well as music parallels that of the white Ball of Love and Beauty. Even though Rena attends the dance, she yearns for George Tryon. She decides that "one must stoop in order that one may lift others" (p. 192). Now neither black nor white, Rena decides to leave her mother and Patesville to teach Negro children who clearly are her intellectual and social inferiors. Her "desire to be of service to her rediscovered people" (p. 175) soon becomes a "discouraging sense of the insignificance of any part she could perform towards the education of three million people with a school term of two months a year" (p. 241). Her idealism frustrated, Rena finds herself pursued both by Jefferson Wain, a mulatto whose intentions are clearly lecherous, and by George Tryon, who does not seem clearly to know his own intentions. Rena can accept neither. Nor can she be rescued by Frank Fowler, the totally faithful, devoted, former slave who dearly loves her. Rena dies of physical exhaustion caused by her flight from both Wain and Tryon. But her physical death is merely an emblem of her destruction as a human being, the result of the painfully acquired knowledge which prevents her from being white and her own inner being which will not allow her to be anything else.

The end of man is knowledge, Robert Penn Warren tells us, but we do not know whether knowledge will save or destroy us. John Walden is transformed by knowledge into John Warwick, an identity he unquestioningly values despite both the destruction of his sister and his knowledge that at least one white gentleman shares his secret. Rena Walden is ultimately destroyed by knowledge. Trapped between two worlds, her knowledge of who and what she is prevents her from belonging to either. As John's role-playing and Rena's melodramatic death suggest, neither alternative is very attractive.

The convolutions of plot and large numbers of characters almost preclude an adequate synopsis of Chesnutt's *The Marrow of Tradition*. This novel presents the racial situation through the linked experiences of two half-sisters, their friends and families during the 1898 race riot in Wilmington, North Carolina.[13] The elder sister is Olivia Merkell Carteret, the white daughter of Samuel and Elizabeth Merkell. She is married to Major Carteret, scion of "one of the oldest and proudest" families in the state. Hopelessly impoverished by the war, Carteret restores the family fortune through his marriage to Olivia. He is now the publisher of the leading newspaper in the state and a noted champion of white supremacy.

The younger sister is Janet Miller, the mulatto daughter of Samuel Merkell and his wife's maid, Julia. Although the documents proving it were destroyed at Merkell's death, Janet's father and mother were legally married. Cheated of her inheritance, Janet is as legitimate an heir in all respects as Olivia. The sisters look enough alike to be twins and are often mistaken for each other. Janet is married to Dr. William Miller, the mulatto son of a free Negro sufficiently affluent to send his son North to medical school. Dr. Miller has returned to the South to build a Negro hospital on the site of a plantation mansion destroyed in the Civil War. He, Janet, and their one son live in the old mansion lost by the Carteret family after the war.

As the novel opens, Olivia has just given birth to a boy, the long awaited Carteret son and heir. When the novel closes, the Miller son has been killed in the race riot fomented by Carteret's newspaper; the Carteret son lies near death and can be saved by an operation which only Miller is in a position to perform. There is a melodramatic confrontation between the Carterets and the Millers in which Major Carteret begs the doctor and Olivia begs Janet for the life of their son. Emblematic of Chesnutt's attitude toward the entire racial mess are a young doctor's words to Miller as he heads up the stairs to operate on his wife's nephew: "There's time enough, but none to spare" (p. 329).

Caught up in the racial tragedy of Wellington are characters who represent the full range of southern life. There are white aristocratic gentlemen of the old school and their scapegrace heirs, white trash bigots, ineffectual white moderates, Jewish merchants, and visiting northerners. There are Aunt Jemimas and Uncle Toms, new Negroes male and female whose anger and frustration are a potential source of danger within the community, and black retainers of real dignity who are in every sense themselves southern gentlefolk. There are a few middle-class blacks, educated men who have become doctors and lawyers. Like the characters in a Dickens novel, all of these figures are touched by the social forces which control the novel, all of them are caught up in the catastrophe of the race riot.

As Robert Bone has pointed out in *The Negro Novel in America*, Chesnutt and other early black writers adopted the melodramatic plot from the popular literature of their day. It is the plot of the Scotts, the Hardys, the Dickenses, and the Bulwers gone to seed. It is also the plot, planted and germinating, of southern writers to come, of the Faulkners, the Warrens, the Styrons, the McCullerses. We tend to overlook the melodramatic, the sentimental, the coincidental in many white southern writers because these qualities are overlaid with poetic rhetoric, with the symbolic. In the highly melodramatic *All the King's Men*, for example, Jack Burden's story turns on solving the mystery of his parentage. Consider the number of chance meetings in Faulkner's *Light in August*, or, better yet, the number of guns throughout Faulkner which have failed to go off at point-blank range. More to the point, Robert N. Farnsworth has commented on the similarity between Chesnutt's "family tragedy, marked by alienation of sisters due to racial bigotry" in *The Marrow of Tradition* and Faulkner's Sutpen family tragedy in *Absalom, Absalom!* In both the "alienation within the family is microcosmic. It symbolizes the bitter and unnatural gulf between black and white men and women who have a blood kinship which their cultural situation will not permit them to recognize."[14] Although Farnsworth does not say so, Major Carteret's return to a devastated South and bankrupt state, his exchange of his family name for Olivia's family wealth, and his longing for a son are all genteel manifestations of the same impulse which drove Colonel Sutpen to try to restore the ruined Sutpen's Hundred, to breed a son with either Rosa Coldfield or Millie Jones, and, finally, to accept a semisuicidal death. The symbolism implicit in the new Negro hospital on the site of a ruined antebellum mansion, or the black doctor residing in the old Carteret mansion, or the black sibling cheated of an inheritance is clearly of a kind with the more complex, thoroughgoing symbolism developed by Faulkner or Warren or Styron.

It is not, however, simply the use of melodramatic plots or occasional symbols which suggests Chesnutt's kinship with white southern authors, especially those of this century. A number of ideas, motifs, and themes are explicitly present in *The Marrow of Tradition* which are the stock in trade of numerous southern novelists, early and later. A concern with the past is one of these. As C. Hugh Holman notes in *The Immoderate Past: The Southern Writer and History*, the southern imagination has been focused on history for almost two hundred years. Early writers such as William Gilmore Sims wrote Sir Walter Scott–like novels to show that the past teaches lessons which can be applied to contemporary lives. Chesnutt's references to *Ivanhoe* in *The House behind the Cedars*, as well as his use of an actual historical episode—the riot at Wilmington—as the central event in *The Marrow of Tradition* suggest a rather deliberate self-identification with the Scott-Sims literary school. Although hardly Sims-like in approach, later writers such as Wolfe, Faulkner, Warren, and Styron also share this early concern with the relationship between time past, present, and future. Chesnutt's interest is implicit in the way he uses the flashback into the past to explain the events in time present. It is suggested symbolically by the presence of the carved font, "which had come from England in the reign of King Charles the Martyr" (p. 12), in which the Carteret baby is baptized. It is further suggested in the moving of the family tombstones but not bodies when the Poindexter place is sold to become the site of a Negro hospital. But Chesnutt also states his concern explicitly. When Dr. Miller sees the continuing anger of black Josh Green over his parents' mistreatment by the K K K, Chesnutt says: "He realized, too, for a moment, the continuity of life, how inseparably the present is woven with the past, how certainly the future will be but the outcome of the present" (p. 112). Not only does this passage generally recall the obsession with time expressed by any number of southern white novelists, it specifically suggests Jack Burden's web theory of life and his realization that he can have no present or future without an understanding of the past. Senile Aunt Polly Ochiltree, one of the most bigoted of the Carteret family retainers, represents a false attitude toward the past. When she sees new construction where the Poindexter mansion once stood, she thinks it is the destroyed past being restored rather than something new being built to benefit the future. When she is corrected, however, she exclaims: "Hugh Poindexter has sold the graves of his ancestors to a negro" (p. 127). Significantly enough, one of the graves has been opened and there is nothing left of the ancestor except a little dust. Only the tombstones, the symbol of the dead past, have been transferred to the white cemetery. A proper understanding of the past and present is specifically attributed to Rena Walden in *The House behind the Cedars*. "To her sensitive spirit to-day was born of yesterday, to-morrow would be but the offspring of to-day" (p. 175). Certainly it is Rena who is unable to deny her past, who must try to go home again, to return to her mother. It is John who says, characteristically enough, "Let the dead past bury its dead" (p. 73).

Rena, like Faulkner's Lena Grove, intuitively gains her understanding of time and the attitude toward life such an understanding implies. It is not a matter she has reasoned through. Along with Faulkner and many other latter-day southern romantics, Chesnutt feels that the human heart is the source of both man's glory and his misery. It is clearly superior to human reason. At one point in *The Marrow of Tradition* he comments: "We speak of the mysteries of inanimate nature. The workings of the human heart are the profoundest mystery of the universe. One moment they make us despair of our kind, and the next we see in them the reflection of the divine image" (p. 233). When he describes Janet Miller's attitude toward her white half-sister, Chesnutt tells us her feelings are mixed. Like Charles Bon waiting for his father, Colonel Sutpen, to acknowledge him, she yearns "for a kind word, a nod, a smile, the least thing that imagination might have twisted into a recognition of the tie between them. . . . When the heart speaks, reason falls into the background, and Janet would have worshiped this sister, even afar off, had she received even the slightest encouragement" (pp. 65–66). Instead, she is—again like Charles Bon—spurned. When at the novel's end Olivia Carteret is forced to acknowledge Janet in order to get Dr. Miller to help save her son's life, Janet spurns the recognition as being too tardy. Janet allows her husband to try to save young Carteret not because he is the son of her sister but because, even as a woman who has been terribly wronged, she can feel sympathy for another human being, even the woman who has wronged her.

Throughout the novel Dr. Miller follows reason, Josh Green emotion. Miller is the highly educated physician who represses his feelings in order to be allowed to heal his people and care for his family. Josh Green is a laborer of great strength, a noble savage of violence waiting to revenge himself on those who have injured him and his parents. When the riot starts, Green asks Miller to lead a band of Negroes in resisting the whites. Miller refuses because the blacks are hopelessly outnumbered and can only be destroyed. He denies himself the satisfaction of the defiant gesture so that he may continue his work. Even though he is convinced that he is acting wisely, he also feels both shame and envy. As he leads the band away, the more impetuous Green says, "Come along, boys! . . . I'd rather be a dead nigger any day dan a live dog!" (p. 284). As Farnsworth has pointed out, this dramatization of the conflict between the rational desire to survive and the emotional desire for revenge suggests some of the conflict within Chesnutt himself: his mind is with Miller, his emotional impulses are with Green.

Chesnutt includes other truths of the heart which are familiar to students of southern literature. Despite the evil of the southern caste system, despite the forces which act upon him, man lives with free will in a moral universe. In *The House behind the Cedars,* Chesnutt frequently emphasizes that Molly Walden was a free agent and was responsible for her actions. Mink Snopes would recognize a figure very much like his "Old Moster" in Chesnutt's reference to "God, or Fate, or whatever one may choose to call the Power that holds the destinies of man in the hollow of his hand" (p. 253). Willie Stark would agree with Chesnutt's authorial comment that "selfishness is the most constant of human motives" (p. 239). Judith Sutpen would understand Chesnutt's feeling that "we are all puppets in the hand of Fate, and seldom see the strings that move us" (p. 304). Jack Burden and Cass Mastern would both respond to Chesnutt's simile: "As a stone dropped into a pool of water sets in motion a series of concentric circles which disturb the whole mass in varying degree, so Mrs. Ochiltree's enigmatic remark had started in her niece's mind a disturbing train of thought" (p. 132). Ike McCaslin would sympathize with gentlemanly old Mr. Delamere's resumé of slavery: "We thought to overrule God's laws, and we enslaved these people for our greed, and sought to escape the man stealer's curse by laying to our souls the flattering unction that we were making of barbarous negroes civilized and Christian men" (p. 211). Any number of latter-day Southern writers would endorse Chesnutt's judgment and prophecy that "Sins, like chickens, come home to roost. The South paid a fearful price for the wrong of negro slavery: in some form or another it will doubtless reap the fruits of [segregation and disenfranchisement]" (p. 241). And surely Faulkner's "They endured" captures poetically the ideas Chesnutt expresses much more prosaically in the mind of Dr. Miller:

"Was it not, after all, a wise provision of nature that had given to a race, destined to a long servitude and a slow emergence therefrom, a cheerfulness of spirit which enabled them to catch pleasure on the wing, and endure with equanimity the ills that seemed inevitable? The ability to live and thrive under adverse circumstances is the surest guaranty of the future. The race which at the last shall inherit the earth—the residuary legatee of civilization—will be the race which remains longest upon it." (pp. 61–62)

Chesnutt clearly is not among the great writers of the South. His plots are weak, not because they are melodramatic, but because the melodrama is so transparent; his characterizations are inadequate, not because they are stereotypes, but because they are bloodless stereotypes; his "message" lacks impact, not because it is trite, but because it is not embodied within the mythos of his story. His diction is wooden, his dialogue unrealistic, his effects strained. But he is clearly a southern writer. Not only is his subject matter southern, his interests and impulses are southern. His message is racial tolerance. His deepest concern is with an individual's attempt to achieve identity after the old order has been destroyed and before the new one has yet been clearly defined. He sees man as a morally free agent confronting forces and impulses that he cannot control. While he lacks a sense of either the truly comic or the truly tragic which informs the writings of his literary betters, Chesnutt also lacks despair. His work, in the words of Saunders Redding, "is fed by the same roots sunk into the same cultural soil" as the writings of his white southern colleagues. Not a great novelist, Chesnutt was a great southerner; he belongs within the southern literary tradition.

III

Themes and Cadences
James Weldon Johnson, 1871–1938

Johnson was a Southerner, and the life-style he eventually carried to New York and around the world was Southern. And the cadences of his poetry and the themes of his prose are Southern.

—Saunders Redding,
"James Weldon Johnson (1871–1938)"

The life which James Weldon Johnson describes in *Along This Way*[1] is that of a highly talented man to whom writing was a serious but secondary interest. Johnson's primary interest was the work of the NAACP, and from 1916 until 1930 he was the field secretary of that organization. But even this work failed to consume him. During his sixty-seven years James Weldon Johnson had many interests and several careers. Born in 1871 in Jacksonville, Florida, he served for a time as the principal of a grammar school there; he was the founding editor of *The Daily American*, the first Negro daily newspaper; he was admitted to the Florida Bar in 1897; by the early 1900s he and his brother, Rosamond, were writing successful Broadway musicals; he served as consul to Venezuela during the administrations of Presidents Roosevelt and Taft; he compiled *The Book of American Negro Poetry* (1922) and *The Book of American Negro Spirituals* (with Rosamond, in 1925), created the seven Negro sermons in verse that make up *God's Trombones* (1927), and wrote his autobiography, *Along This*

Way (1933). He also wrote *The Autobiography of an Ex-Coloured Man* (1912), a novel I wish to examine with some care.

Johnson's later years were filled with honors. He was awarded the Spingarn Medal by the N A A C P for his achievements as "author, diplomat, and public servant." He received the Harmon Award for *God's Trombones* and was elected a trustee of Atlanta University. Both Talledega College and Howard University conferred on him the degree of Litt.D. In 1929 Johnson was awarded a fellowship from the Julius Rosenwald Fund to allow him to devote a year exclusively to writing. In 1930 Johnson became the Adam K. Spence Professor of Creative Literature at Fisk University, a position he held until his death in 1938.

Like Charles Waddell Chesnutt, James Weldon Johnson drew upon both Negro folklore and his own experiences as a southern black for the subject matter of his writing. Chesnutt presented Negro folk tales in his conjure stories; Johnson collected spirituals, and in *God's Trombones* preserved the cadences of the Negro folk sermon. But Johnson was a more restrained, conscious artist than was Chesnutt.[2] Like Joel Chandler Harris, Chesnutt used dialect extensively in his conjure stories and, when depicting the speech of uneducated blacks, in his novels; Johnson avoided dialect because he felt it was looked upon almost exclusively as a source either of pathos or of humor, and these were not the effects he was after.[3] Yet in works such as *God's Trombones*, Johnson clearly suggests southern Negro church speech through his reproduction of the southern black minister's characteristic rhetorical devices—the repetitions, the alliterations, the pauses, the echoes from the King James Bible, the folk images—all of which show that Johnson was as conscious of dialectical nuances as was Twain in writing *The Adventures of Huckleberry Finn* or Faulkner in writing the Rev'un Shegog's Easter sermon in *The Sound and the Fury.* Johnson's ability to create the effect of dialect without using its typical spellings or illiteracies is one of his greatest skills as an artist.

Johnson's fiction evidences a similar skill. Like earlier southern writers black and white—Cable, Twain, Chesnutt—Johnson dramatizes the plight of the mulatto. As with Chesnutt's protagonists in *The House behind the Cedars* and *The Marrow of Tradition*, the central issue confronting the hero of *The Autobiography of an Ex-*

Coloured Man is his identity in a society where racial caste deter-
mines who one is. But here the similarity ends. In spirit and in
form, Johnson's work is much closer to Ellison's *Invisible Man* than
it is to anything by Chesnutt.[4]

The ex-coloured man, like Ellison's protagonist, is the novel's
nameless narrator. Referred to throughout as "I," he is never
named because the naming would reveal his identity to the white
world within which he lives. While Johnson's purpose is to lend
verisimilitude to his narrative, his effect is similar to Ellison's: neither protagonist has an identity. The invisible man's identity is
denied him by a society which will not see him as he is; the ex-coloured man finally denies his own identity as a black when he elects
to "pass" and become "white." Like Ellison's novel, Johnson's is or-
ganized in picaresque fashion around the experiences and perceptions of the narrator. Even the decision to write an autobiography is
informed by the judgment the ex-coloured man passes on himself
and society, suggesting the ironic vision of the invisible man: "Back
of it all, I think I find a sort of savage and diabolical desire to gather
up all the little tragedies of my life, and turn them into a practical
joke on society."[5]

Johnson's "I" was born in Georgia shortly after the Civil War.
Rather than telling the reader that his narrator is black, Johnson has
him recall impressions of the house, the flowers, the glass-bottle
hedge, the wash tubs, the vegetable garden which surrounded him,
the bread and molasses which he ate. In short, he remembers details which tell us that he almost certainly came from a southern
rural Negro home. He also remembers the tall man with the shiny
boots, the gold chain, and the watch, who visited his mother from
time to time and who hung a ten dollar gold piece with a hole
drilled in it around his neck as a gift when the narrator and his
mother moved north to Connecticut. In Connecticut the narrator
demonstrates some musical talent and is given piano lessons. He is
also a good student. He is splendidly happy until one day, when he
is about ten years old, his teacher identifies him as a Negro before
the class. Like many other southern protagonists, black and white,
he is shattered by a knowledge he cannot comprehend. In Faulkner's *Absalom, Absalom!* (1936), Mr. Compson imagines Charles
Etienne de Saint Velery Bon, when he is told "that he was, must be,

a negro," looking at himself in "the shard of broken mirror" during "what hours of amazed and tearless grief . . . examining himself . . . with quiet and incredulous incomprehension." In Johnson's 1912 novel, the protagonist rushes to his room and goes quickly to his looking glass.

For an instant I was afraid to look, but when I did, I looked long and earnestly. . . . I was accustomed to hear remarks about my beauty; but now, for the first time, I became conscious of it and recognized it. I noticed the ivory whiteness of my skin, the beauty of my mouth, the size and liquid darkness of my eyes. . . . I noticed the softness and glossiness of my dark hair. . . . How long I stood there gazing at my image I do not know. . . . I ran downstairs and rushed to where my mother was sitting. . . . I buried my head in her lap and blurted out: "Mother, mother, tell me, am I a nigger?" (p. 17)

He is, in effect, asking his mother who he is. She answers that he is neither a "nigger" nor white; her refusal even to name his father makes his identity even more equivocal. Nameless, raceless, father-less, like the Joe Christmas of Faulkner's *Light in August*, he is a person without a definable self. And also like Christmas, he assumes a racial identity based, as Cleanth Brooks has pointed out, on a state of mind rather than on the possession of Negro genes:[6] "And so I have often lived through that hour, that day, that week, in which was wrought the miracle of my transition from one world into another; for I did indeed pass into another world. From that time I looked out through other eyes, my thoughts were coloured, my words dictated, my actions limited by one dominating, all-pervad-ing idea which constantly increased in force and weight until I fi-nally realized in it a great, tangible fact" (pp. 20–21).

In *Absalom, Absalom!* when Charles Bon learns that he is a Negro, he revenges himself upon Thomas Sutpen, the father who has rejected him, by destroying Sutpen's "Design." Tainted with only the suspicion that he is part Negro, Joe Christmas defies and defiles God and the society which have made him. In contrast, the ex-coloured man accepts the place society allots him. He compen-sates, however, by withdrawing into his books and music. Like Chesnutt's John Walden in *The House behind the Cedars*, Johnson's protagonist gains such solace as he can from his reading. But instead of the southern favorites, Sir Walter Scott and Bulwer-Lytton, it is the northern Harriet Beecher Stowe who shows him "who and what I was and what my country considered me" (p. 42). Even granting Stowe's excesses, *Uncle Tom's Cabin* would appear to offer more realistic guidance to any nineteenth-century American, white or black, than either *Ivanhoe* or *The Last of the Barons*. After he learns about slavery from *Uncle Tom's Cabin*, he can talk with his mother freely about the past and about his white aristocratic father. As it does for Robert Penn Warren's Jack Burden in *All the King's Men*, knowledge of the past helps to define the present. The definition of self gained from indirect and partial knowledge leads to a desire for a fuller, firsthand knowledge. His mother's tales of time past and the "old folks" cause the narrator to want to see the South. And while his South is perhaps not the dark Helen of his blood (as it was for the Eugene Gant of *Look Homeward, Angel*), it is the land of his birth and holds a "peculiar fascination . . . over my imagination" (p. 51).

Music offers a means of both social and economic survival. His early recitals give him status in the community. On the one occasion when his father visits them in Connecticut, the twelve-year-old narrator stirs so much parental pride by playing a Chopin waltz that his father sends him a new upright piano. His ability to play and give lessons on the piano becomes a means of support during a portion of his adult life.

Given some measure of self-definition by his reading, his music, and his discussions with his mother, the narrator becomes not only reconciled to his race but proud of it. He begins to dream of "bringing glory and honour to the Negro race." He wants "to be a great man, a great coloured man" (p. 46). As high school comes to an end, he plans to enter Harvard or Yale. But with the death of his mother, and because he receives no help from his father, the narrator decides to use such money as he has to attend Atlanta University.

The narrator's first trip South is disappointing. Instead of the luxuriant, romantic South of his imagination, he finds red earth covered by tough, scrawny grass, straggling roads, and cottages of unpainted pine. Instead of the public squares and fountains of a typical New England town, he finds the new Atlanta, somewhat like its namesake, "drowning, or, rather, suffocating in the mud" (p. 53). Instead of being inspired to admiration by Stowean darkies, he is repelled by the unkempt, shambling, slouching, loud Negroes whom he meets; he is attracted only by their dialect and hearty laughter. Like Ellison's invisible man and almost all of Chesnutt's protagonists, Johnson's narrator has not only accepted the white man's stereotype of the black, but also the white man's judgment of him. And like the invisible man, who wants to reject his southern heritage by having a Yankee breakfast but then affirms it when he buys a yam from a sidewalk vendor, Johnson's protagonist finds a valid basis for identifying himself with the South when he eats a breakfast of southern fried chicken, boiled hominy, and biscuits, thereby realizing at least "one of my dreams of Southern life" (p. 59).

Robbed of his savings by a black train porter, the narrator cannot attend Johnson's alma mater. He goes instead to Johnson's home town, where he lands a job in a tobacco factory and teaches music in his spare time. Like Wolfe's Altamont, Faulkner's Jefferson, or Twain's St. Petersburg, Johnson's Jacksonville is the place of his youth; the life he describes is the life he knew as a boy growing up in the South. It both is and is not like the faraway country which Louis Rubin describes. For Rubin, southern writers fall into two broad categories. Those who wrote before the Civil War are primarily men of letters rather than imaginative artists. They usually are lawyers, clergymen, or physicians who also write. They accept the fundamental values and ethos of southern society.[7] Later came the imaginative artists whose vision forced them to question the values and assumptions of the South. Like Thomas Mann's Tonio Kröger, they are, somehow, both in and apart from the society which produced them.

Johnson straddles both groups. Certainly his career as a lawyer, teacher, librettist, and NAACP leader affirms his interest and involvement in the crucial events of his time. His descriptions, both in his novel and his autobiography, of black middle-class family life place high value on the family (father as well as mother), church life, hard work, and education as a means of upward mobility. That is, he affirms almost every aspect of the traditional southern white ethic except its attitude toward blacks. And of course a rejection of the southern racial caste system is one of the characteristics which separate modern writers such as Twain, Faulkner, Styron, Mc-

Cullers, and Warren from the white culture which produced them. Unlike the southern white writers, who in some measure elect to stand outside their culture, however, the black Johnson is an unwilling outcast from full participation in all aspects of southern life.[8] He is both a part of southern society and apart from it. While I cannot prove cause and effect, the result seems to be a curious coupling of the life and works of the old-fashioned southern man of letters with that of the southern writer since Twain, who questions and rejects some of the traditional values of southern life.

At the tobacco factory the narrator learns not only to make cigars, but, like Johnson himself, "to smoke, to swear, and to speak Spanish." Through his music teaching he "became acquainted with the best class of coloured people in Jacksonville. This was really my entrance into the race. It was my initiation into what I . . . termed the free-masonry of the race," an initiation that allowed him to see "the tremendous struggle . . . going on between the races in the South" (pp. 74–75). The purpose of this struggle is to hold the Negro back, to keep him in his place. And to a degree the struggle succeeds. For the black man uses much of his creative energy resisting, however passively. The white man, however, is also held back. For he too consumes his best energies in the struggle. The effect on the white southerner (at least until recently) is that he has lost his place of leadership in the nation as a whole; the effect on the black southerner is that he is divided into three groups: those like Bigger Thomas, Joe Christmas, and the malevolent Will of Styron's *The Confessions of Nat Turner*, who cherish a sullen hatred for all whites and lash out in violence at the least excuse; those like Uncle Tom and Dilsey, who work as servants and lead gentle, kindhearted, wholesome, religious lives; and those like Chesnutt's Dr. Miller, Faulkner's Lucas Beauchamp, and Carson McCullers's Dr. Copeland (*The Heart Is a Lonely Hunter*) who violate the accepted stereotypes by virtue of their independence, their money, their education, or their cultural attainments. This last group contains the "uppity niggers" who refuse to accept the places traditionally allotted to them.

Johnson does not dramatize either the enraged or the subservient black in his novel. His true interest and subject matter is the independent Negro middle class; that is, his own class. His narrator's entrance into the freemasonry of the race is actually his entry into respectable Negro society. Through his narrator, Johnson becomes an apologist for this group, commenting approvingly on its social excursions, public balls, church socials, and music.[9] Indeed, the narrator is about to take a permanent place within the Jacksonville black community when the cigar factory is closed.

The factory shutdown, like the death of the narrator's mother or the loss of his savings, is another of the obviously fortuitous accidents by which Johnson moves his narrator along on his semipicaresque journey. The narrator quickly gives up his plan to marry a young school teacher, raise a family, and live respectably in Jacksonville for the rest of his life. Instead he goes north to New York, where he enters the world of pool playing, gambling, and jazz. He becomes a ragtime pianist and supports himself by playing at black clubs and white social gatherings. He leaves this milieu as quickly as he enters it; a white deus ex machina who likes him and his playing takes him to Paris.

He spends his time there studying French, seeing the sights, and attending the opera. Like a latter-day Moll Flanders discovering one of her former husbands in prison, the narrator suddenly discovers that he is sitting by his father and half-sister during a performance of Gounod's "Faust." Already attracted to the beautiful girl next to him, the narrator experiences an almost overwhelming sense of affection for a sister he cannot approach. He wants to fall worshipfully at her feet, but cannot because of the blood tie; he wants to touch her hand and call her sister, but he knows he cannot reveal himself in this way. Almost suffocating, he leaves the theater and gets drunk. The situation is perhaps comparable to that of Charles Bon when he finds himself in his father's Mississippi home courting his own half-sister. Faulkner, however, universalizes Charles Bon's plight to the point of tragedy by forcing Quentin Compson, Shreve McCannon, and the reader to project themselves into Bon's mind as each tries to recreate the past. Johnson, on the other hand, merely states that his narrator's plight is "a real tragedy." With Gounod's music playing softly in the background, the effect, appropriately enough, is merely pathetic, not tragic. Although the result is a lesser achievement by a lesser artist than Faulkner, the black-white blood tie and the brother-sister passion in both *Absalom* and the

Autobiography certainly suggest parallel visions of the actual relationship between southern blacks and whites.

While in Europe, the narrator sees a way to fulfill his childhood ambition of becoming a great coloured man. He decides to return home, "to go back into the very heart of the South" (p. 142), and transform Negro folk materials into classical forms that would both reveal their worth and help preserve them. When the narrator's patron learns of this purpose, he tries to persuade the narrator that his intention is quixotic. The patron, who throughout the novel has been described as a man trying to escape, to bridge over, or to blot out time, argues that since evil is a force which cannot be annihilated, the best one can do is seek such personal happiness as one can find. He feels that only misery can result from someone with the white appearance, education, and tastes of the narrator throwing his life away amid the poverty, ignorance, and hopeless struggle of black people. As an ironic commentary on his own attempt to escape both personal misery and time, this hedonistic patron eventually commits suicide.

In contrast to his patron's self-destructive hedonism is the benevolent theism of the ex-slave whom the narrator meets on his return voyage to New York. The ex-slave's present status as a free, cultured man, a physician graduated from Howard University, is visible proof that the condition of the race is not hopeless. His faith that "there is a principle of right in the world, which finally prevails," and "a merciful justice-loving god in heaven" sustains his belief that racial justice will eventually prevail (pp. 151–52). It also philosophically justifies the narrator's plan to return to his people.

Neither Johnson's passing comments on time nor his assertions of a moral purpose in the universe can be considered profound. They are, however, part and parcel of the southern writer's philosophical baggage. Faulkner's Ike McCaslin and V. K. Ratliff both affirm that it is indeed a moral universe. So do Warren's Jack Burden and Willie Stark, Styron's Nat Turner, and Flannery O'Connor's almost everybody. While Johnson—like most other southern writers—intellectually rejected the southern Protestantism of his youth, his writings—again like those of most other southern writers—affirmed Protestant patterns of conduct and Protestant moral attitudes. In short, while not profoundly philosophical, Johnson's comments are profoundly southern.

Some of Johnson's comments also suggest at least a sympathy for stereotypical southern whites and their attitudes. Moreover, he sees a fundamental similarity between white and black southerners in that both defend their vices as well as their virtues. While on the train from Nashville to Atlanta, Johnson's narrator observes a Jewish businessman, a university professor from Ohio, an old Union veteran, and a Texas cotton planter as they begin to converse. The narrator comments that southerners are more unreservedly gregarious than northerners, that they not only must talk, but must express their opinions. Whether or not this is true, it is certainly a southern notion. And after listening to a discussion of race in which the Texan takes an ignorantly bigoted position, the narrator admits to feeling

a certain sort of admiration for the man who could not be swayed from what he felt he held as his principles. . . . All along, in spite of myself, I have been compelled to accord the same kind of admiration to the Southern white man for the manner in which he defends not only his virtues, but his vices. He knows that, judged by a high standard, he is narrow and prejudiced, that he is guilty of unfairness, oppression, and cruelty, but this he defends as stoutly as he would his better qualities. This same spirit obtains in a great degree among the blacks; they, too, defend their faults and failings. . . . It is the spirit of the South to defend everything belonging to it. (p. 165)

Through his narrator, Johnson even accepts the conventional view of most white southerners that whereas northern whites love the Negro as an abstraction, a race, but have no particular liking for individual Negroes, southern whites despise the Negro race, but have a strong affection for its individual members.

Once more in the South, the narrator begins to gather the Negro folk materials he intends to preserve and publish, including folk songs and sermons collected at Negro revival meetings; that is, the same materials Johnson himself collected and published ten to fifteen years later in *The Book of American Negro Spirituals* and *God's Trombones*. Indeed, the narrator's depiction of a black preacher's sermon includes the line, "Young man, your arm's too

short to box with God!" (p. 178). Johnson used the same line to begin his verse sermon "The Prodigal Son" in *God's Trombones*. The
point is not that Johnson repeated himself (so did Faulkner and
Wolfe, among others), nor that his imagination rendered the same
subject matter into both prose and poetry (as did the imaginations
of other southern writers), but that Johnson saw in southern evangelical black Protestantism a major portion of both the source and
the embodiment of southern black culture. Obviously southern
white Protestantism has not been so exclusively wedded to white
folk culture as the church has been to the total black experience.
But the church, especially in the rural South, remains the single
most important source of community identity for white and black
southerner alike. The importance of his churches in the community
and his evangelical Protestantism identify the southerner whether
he be black or white.

At the very time he is collecting materials which affirm the cultural value of his race, the narrator sees a Negro lynched. He is
filled with humiliation and shame at belonging to a race which could
be so treated. He decides that "to forsake one's race to better one's
condition [is] no less worthy an action than to forsake one's country
for the same purpose" (p. 190). He returns to New York and becomes a successful white man. No longer an artist or collector of folk
culture, he becomes the prototypical white American businessman.
He attends business school, saves his money, becomes a slum land-
lord and real estate speculator. He moves socially upward to "a
grade of society of no small degree of culture." He falls in love with
and courts "the most dazzlingly white thing" he had ever seen (pp.
197–98). Although she knows he is an "ex-coloured man," she marries him and bears him a son and a daughter.

Yet despite "making it," he looks upon himself with some ironic
detachment. He sees his very existence as a practical joke played on
white society. And although he professes to love a lily-white wife,
his marriage simply extends the joke. But Johnson clearly intends
that the joke is also on the narrator. When his wife dies, his sole
ambition is to keep his children untainted by his race. And when he
sees Booker T. Washington in New York, he feels like a coward, a
deserter, a traitor to his people. He sees that Washington and others are men making history while he is "an ordinarily successful

white man who has made a little money" (p. 211). He has become the thing suggested by his white father's first gift to him: a ten-dollar gold piece with a hole drilled in it. The coin proclaims its value, but it is essentially worthless because much of its substance is gone. We last see Johnson's narrator surrounded by the symbols of what he might have become—the "fast yellowing manuscripts, the only tangible remnants of a vanished dream, a dead ambition, a sacrificed talent." He is a man who sold his "birthright for a mess of pottage" (p. 211).

Unlike his protagonist, Johnson became a great coloured man. He also became a better than fair writer. Like Charles Waddell Chesnutt before him, his major concern is the plight of the southern Negro. He avoids Chesnutt's sentimentality and melodramatic plotting, however, through the use of an anti-heroic, sometimes ironic first-person narrator. Better than Chesnutt, Johnson describes the experiences and aspirations of middle-class southern blacks. He also begins to suggest that the relationship between blacks and whites is not just a southern problem. At his worst, Johnson is plodding and pedantic. At his best—that is, when he describes a revival meeting or reproduces a Negro sermon—the cadences of his poetry and the themes of his prose not only are black and southern, they are also very good art.

IV

Song of the South
Jean Toomer, 1894–1967

O land and soil, red soil and sweet-gum tree,
So scant of grass, so profligate of pines,
Now just before an epoch's sun declines
Thy son, in time, I have returned to thee,
Thy son, I have in time returned to thee.
—Jean Toomer,
"Song of the Son"

These lines might well have been written by that laureate of the South, Sidney Lanier; instead, they are from Jean Toomer's *Cane*, a work as difficult to define as its author. Both the man and his work contain a multitude of self-contradictions. Toomer was and was not a Negro; was and was not a southerner; indeed, was and was not Jean Toomer. *Cane* is and is not a novel; is and is not verse; is and is not drama. Both man and work are both more and less than all of these. And as Darwin Turner has shown, both man and work are fully comprehensible only in terms of each other.[1]

Nathan Eugene Toomer was born in that most ambiguously southern of cities, Washington, D.C., in 1894. His father, Nathan Toomer, came from Georgia and returned to that state when he deserted his wife and child. His mother, Nina Pinchback Toomer, was the daughter of P. B. S. Pinchback, a Georgia-born Afro-American who became lieutenant governor of Louisiana during Reconstruction. Young Toomer was reared in the Pinchback household and, ex-

38

cept for a brief time in New York City, lived in Washington, D.C., from his birth until 1914, when he went away to college. Even though he strongly resented his stern and domineering grandfather, such identity as he had was so determined by his mother's father that for a while he was even known as Eugene Pinchback. As a college student, Toomer added ambiguity of race and uncertainty of purpose to his other identity problems. According to Turner, Toomer feared that he would be rejected by his fellow students if they knew his ancestry. Therefore, he began what was to become his lifelong pattern of being either ambiguous or evasive about his race. Between 1914 and 1917 he studied agriculture at the University of Wisconsin, physical education at the American College of Physical Training in Chicago, premedicine at the University of Chicago, sociology at New York University, and history at C.C.N.Y. Rejected by the army during World War I because of poor eyesight and a hernia, Toomer worked as an automobile salesman in Chicago, a substitute physical education director in Milwaukee, a grocery clerk and (very briefly) a shipyard laborer in New York, all before the end of 1919. During this time he was converted from Christianity to atheism back to an unorthodox theism and from capitalism to socialism back to capitalism. He had also been converted more permanently to literature and to the intellectual life.

In 1920 Toomer gained some independence from work and from his grandfather as a result of a $600 legacy from his mother. He was free to read widely and to make the acquaintance of such literary figures as Edwin Arlington Robinson, Waldo Frank, Lola Ridge, and—later—Malcolm Cowley, Van Wyck Brooks, Hart Crane, Kenneth Burke, and Robert Littell. He was also free to redefine himself as writer and artist and to rename himself Jean Toomer.

None of Toomer's earliest work was published, and only a play and the fragments of an autobiographical novel survive. Both of these, according to Turner, argue the case of the repressed American Negro. That is to say, they work more or less the same vein of social criticism already mined by Charles Waddell Chesnutt and James Weldon Johnson. Then in 1921 the twenty-seven-year-old Toomer spent three months as temporary head of a Negro industrial school in Sparta, Georgia. There, like Johnson's ex-coloured man, he was initiated into the freemasonry of his racial past. He discovered that although born and reared in Washington, D.C., his roots were in the deep South; that although he had been educated in the East and Midwest, his entire being responded to the rural South. Thus he discovered, at least for a time, that his true subject matter was the southern land, its people, its ethos; and he discovered that the lyrical voice of a poet in prose was the proper means of expressing his response to his people and his past.

Before he went to Georgia, Toomer could not have known the extent to which he was a southerner; after the visit, he could not escape this knowledge. In 1923 he published the sketches, poems, stories, and dramatic pieces which make up *Cane*. He also wrote a brief autobiographical sketch that stresses his southern roots: "My family is from the South. My mother's father, P. B. S. Pinchback, born in Macon, Georgia, left home as a boy and worked on the Mississippi River steamers. . . . My own father likewise came from Middle Georgia." In this same sketch Toomer openly discussed his ambiguous racial identity and his self-identification at that time with Negroes and the South:

Racially, I seem to have (who knows for sure) seven blood mixtures: French, Dutch, Welsh, Negro, German, Jewish, and Indian. Because of these, my position in America has been a curious one. I have lived equally amid the two race groups. Now white, now colored. From my own point of view I am naturally and inevitably an American. . . . Within the last two or three years, however, my growing need for artistic expression has pulled me deeper and deeper into the Negro group. And as my powers of receptivity increased, I found myself loving it in a way that I could never love the other. . . . A visit to Georgia last fall was the starting point of almost everything of worth that I have done. I heard folk-songs come from the lips of Negro peasants. I saw the rich dusk beauty that I had heard many false accents about, and of which till then, I was somewhat skeptical. And a deep part of my nature, a part that I had repressed, sprang suddenly to life and responded to them.[2]

For a brief moment Jean Toomer's sense of himself as a southerner, a Negro, and an artist fused in such a way that he could write and live effectually. Within a few short months this fusion had dissolved. In the summer of 1923 he urged his publisher not to advertise *Cane* as the work of a Negro (this despite Waldo Frank's introduction proclaiming Toomer's ancestry). In 1927 he wrote of himself as neither black nor white but as a human being who belonged to both groups. In 1930, according to Turner, he refused to allow James Weldon Johnson to include any of his work in *The Book of American Negro Poetry.* In 1931 he stated in the privately published *A Fiction and Some Facts* that "as for being a Negro, this of course, I am not—neither biologically nor socially."[3] Concomitant with this repudiation of racial identity was a loss of his sense of being a southerner.

Also in 1923 Toomer came under the influence of Georges Ivanovitch Gurdjieff. This guru envisioned and preached a progression of experiences from self-consciousness to cosmic awareness. Toomer became an evangelist for Gurdjieff; he turned from writing works that had recognizable literary merit to using forms designed to embody his new vision of life. Lacking the talent of either a Milton or a Blake, Toomer could not publish his visionary works. Only one play and a handful of essays, stories, and poems appeared between *Cane* in 1923 and his death in 1967. He left three unpublished novels, four unpublished plays, eight unpublished philosophical pieces, two unpublished volumes of poetry, six unpublished stories, and four unpublished autobiographies.

Whatever else Toomer became at some later time, in 1922, when he was writing *Cane,* he clearly thought of himself as a southerner and identified himself with the Negro portion of his racial heritage. Whether or not he thought of himself as a novelist is less clear. Darwin Turner denies that Toomer was a novelist at this time, because, he asserts, *Cane* is not a novel, not even an experimental novel, but simply a "collection of character sketches, short stories, poems, and a play, which forms one of the most distinguished achievements in the writings of Americans." Turner supports his contention by arguing that Toomer composed the pieces separately, sent them individually to various editors, and wrote Waldo Frank that he "had the impulse to collect [his] sketches and poems under the title perhaps of *Cane.*" Turner further notes that various publishers wanted Toomer to send them a novel rather than another book like *Cane.*[4]

Paradoxically enough, a writer is sometimes considered a novelist only after the fact. Defoe and Richardson are obvious cases in point. Fielding's comic epic poems in prose are judged as novels, not as epics or poems. This is because, rightly or wrongly, we consider the works of these early writers within the context of the later development of prose fiction. Turner makes light of Robert Bone's description of Toomer as a poet-novelist and of *Cane* as an important Negro novel because evidence shows that Toomer did not think of *Cane* as a novel. But surely Bone is correct in seeing affinities between *Cane* and the experimental work of a Stein or a Hemingway or an Anderson.[5] That Toomer submitted his pieces separately before collecting them in *Cane* seems irrelevant. Writing after Toomer, Faulkner did the same with various parts of *Go Down, Moses* and *The Unvanquished.* And even though Faulkner thought of *Go Down, Moses* as a novel, and it is so considered today, that work was first published as *Go Down, Moses and Other Stories*—a fact which at least suggests how Faulkner's publisher thought of the work—and was initially received as a collection of stories. On the other hand, Faulkner seems to have conceived of *The Unvanquished* as a series of stories, even though today it is published as "a novel by William Faulkner." And whatever Faulkner's view, Michael Millgate, Cleanth Brooks, Hyatt H. Waggoner, Carvel Collins, and James B. Meriwether—that is, a virtual pantheon of Faulkner critics—agree that *The Unvanquished* is a novel.[6]

Perhaps Richard S. Kennedy is correct when he asks us to accept a new rubric identifying works which defy easy generic classification. His unhappy term is "fictional thesaurus."

A fictional thesaurus is a long literary work made up of short units of prose or verse in which the parts are joined together by association of ideas rather than by probable and necessary development. It displays a mixture of styles and variations in mood but, taken together, presents a coherent thematic statement or view of life. It achieves unity by its association with the actions of a single character or a closely related group of characters and sometimes by the voice of a single narrator or spokeman. . . .

Thus Wolfe's *Of Time and the River* can be placed in the same company with other works that have always caused generic difficulty, such as Waldo Frank's *City Block*, Joyce's *Ulysses*, Dos Passos' *U.S.A.*, Cummings' *Eimi*, Huxley's *Ape and Essence*, and Jean Toomer's *Cane.*[7]

Perhaps "fictional thesaurus" is indeed the term to describe Toomer's *Cane*, a series of lyrical vignettes in prose and verse depicting black life in Georgia and in Washington, D.C. The vignettes, as Robert Bone and Darwin Turner have pointed out, are connected by recurrent thematic and lyrical patterns. Since we have not yet developed a critical apparatus for dealing with the comparatively small body which constitutes that genre, it seems reasonable to me to consider *Cane* and *U.S.A.* and *Of Time and the River* and *Ulysses* as experiments in fictional form, and to treat them as experimental novels, no matter what their respective authors did or did not think they were creating.

The episodic structure which makes *Cane* difficult to categorize generically makes it almost impossible to summarize linearly. Even such episodic works as *Winesburg, Ohio* and *Of Time and the River* have a more obviously coherent structure than *Cane*. Like Anderson's vignettes, Toomer's apparently are about a variety of characters. In reality, however, they serve as commentaries on the experiences and perceptions of several young men, all of whom are trying to find an identity for themselves and to understand the world of people with whom they live. And like Wolfe's protagonists, Toomer's are scarcely disguised autobiographical personae. In part one, Toomer presents the impressionistic responses of an outsider, a young black much like himself, to lives and scenes set in a romantically vital rural South. In part two, Toomer presents the entrapment of a number of sensitive young blacks, also much like himself, who live in urban Washington, D.C. Finally, in "Kabnis" Toomer depicts a spiritually paralyzed urban black who is visiting Georgia to teach the rural blacks, as Toomer himself had recently done. The tension between Ralph Kabnis's awareness of black southern life and his inability either to share or shape it gives Toomer's final section as well as the entire work its thematic structure.

The search for identity is, of course, a typically American quest. From Huck Finn to Eugene Gant to Jack Burden to Nat Turner, it is a particular concern of white southern writers. It is also the concern of all major black writers, northern or southern. The search for identity undertaken by Toomer in *Cane* suggests the excruciating ambiguity of the blacks' identity in America. Are they principally American or Negro? Rural peasant or ghetto dweller? Proletarian or bourgeois? What are the costs of either keeping or relinquishing their ethnic identity? Such problems are only superficially different from those of the southern white, at least until very recently. Are they Americans or southerners? Are they loyal agrarians or members of the new industrial South? What are the costs to white southerners of relinquishing their regional identity? The obvious and crucial difference between the southern white and the southern black is, of course, that it has been easier for the white southerner to "pass" into the prevailing national culture. But the fundamental questions are essentially the same, the problems explored and the answers given by Toomer and many of his white confreres frequently identical.

In the first and last sections of *Cane*—that is, those set in the rural South—Toomer wrestles with the identity problem partly through a character's identification with or estrangement from a life-giving earth. Generally speaking, the women are vital, Lena Grove–like earth mothers, certain of their identities. They become beautiful but damned Eula Varners because the men they encounter are inadequate. Like the black Ella Corpening in *Look Homeward, Angel,* who dances nakedly before the paralyzed, inarticulate, adolescent Eugene Gant, the women in *Cane* are figures whose recognized vitality is consistently responded to with an inadequate sexuality by men who are identityless and paralyzed. The first section is filled with crippled Faulkerian fertility figures whose sexuality is as much a part of nature as the sun or the soil. Karintha carries beauty "perfect as dusk when the sun goes down."[8] Like Eula Varner of Faulkner's *The Hamlet* a decade later, Karintha is longed for by all the males in the community. She smiles and indulges them, but her essential feeling (again, like Eula's) is one of indifference approaching contempt. Carma is "pungent and composite." The "smell of farmyards is the fragrance of the woman. She does not sing; her body is a song. She is in the forest, dancing" (p. 17). Just as Faulkner was to use images of nature and allusions to a Western pagan past to suggest that Lena and Eula are fertility figures, so Toomer uses images of nature and references to African witchcraft. "Torches flare . . . juju men, greegree, witch-doctors . . . torches go out. . . . The Dixie Pike has grown from a goat path in Africa" (pp. 17–18). Living by the Pike, Carma has many men. Her husband, unable to cope with her promiscuity, is in prison for slashing a man. Fern, into whose eyes "the whole countryside seemed to flow" and whose "eyes desired nothing that you could give her," also finds the men who surround her inadequate (pp. 24–25, 27). It is not only the Georgia blacks who are inadequate. The Toomer-like narrator from Washington, who, like Eugene Gant responding to a South that "burned like dark Helen in his blood," is inspired by the "soil of [his] ancestors" and emotionally moved by Fern. Yet he can only cause her to spring up and rush away uttering inarticulate sounds. Louisa, who has a color like oak leaves, breasts like ripe acorns, and a singing voice like murmuring winds in the fig trees, is fought over by her black and white lovers. As her black lover is burned for killing her white one, she sits indifferently under the full moon.

If those who are close to the rural soil live lives of marred vitality, those who have left the soil for urban Washington endure a living death. In a Washington filled with Prohibition-rich bootleggers wearing silver shirts and driving zooming Cadillacs, Rhobert is described as sinking into a suffocating mud, the water of his life draining away. With only his own rickety legs to stand on, Rhobert is pushed into the mud by a monstrous stuffed, dead house that he wears on his head. As narrator, Toomer bitterly tells us that God built the house and that Rhobert accepts it and his weak legs as a part of the nature of things. "Like most other men who wear monstrous helmets, the pressure it exerts is enough to convince him of its practical infinity. . . . It is a sad thing," the narrator says, "to see a banty-bowed, shaky, ricket-legged man straining the raw insides of his throat against smooth air" (p. 74). In this Kafkaesque sketch, Rhobert represents all black men destroyed by an urban setting. More, he has accepted the dead structure which traps him. His spiritual imprisonment is so complete that he loses any concern for his wife and children. Since God built the house, we must blame this malevolent deity for such a world. Or, although Toomer does not say so, we might blame a "white power structure" that has created an urban world in which the black man is so cut off from the soil and its life-giving water that his roots there must wither and die. Whatever the original cause, Rhobert's spiritual destruction is directly related to the loss of a Jeffersonian agrarian world in which man's closeness to the soil sustains his humanity.

Seven years before Ransom, Davidson, Tate, and Warren were to take their southern agrarian stands, Toomer was showing that once the initial relationship between man and nature had been destroyed or even seriously impaired, man's spiritual life as embodied in the play of his imagination, his ability to love and enjoy a family, and his very sense of freedom and life were all destroyed. Seven years before Faulkner supposedly invented the modern southern Gothic in "A Rose for Emily" to express the spiritual decay of a southern people who had forgotten or deliberately glamorized the past and thus lost their roots, Toomer followed his own southern Gothic impulses to suggest the distortions inflicted upon a rootless southern black. Thirteen years before Faulkner depicted the moral and spiritual horrors leading to the fall of the house of Sutpen, Toomer depicted the moral and spiritual horror of life for the black man in urban Washington, D.C.

Twenty-five years before Truman Capote's Joel Knox searched for certainty and identity in *Other Voices, Other Rooms* and found instead that he was entrapped in a haunted house sinking into the Louisiana swamp, Toomer's Rhobert had lost all sense of himself except that imposed by the house on his head and had sunk into the mud. Indeed, Capote's description of Joel Knox's experience could fit Rhobert exactly: "'We're sinking, you know, sank four inches last year.' It was drowning in the earth, this house, and they, all of them, were submerging with it." This is not to say that Faulkner, Wolfe, and Capote were influenced directly by Toomer. Rather, all of them were responding to those qualities and values of southern agrarian life whose loss creates a perversion of the human spirit seen and responded to by sensitive men, black and white, as they attempt to create art out of their perceptions and experiences.

If Rhobert is Toomer's principal example of the uprooted urban black, others also exemplify the type. Avey, like her rural sisters Karintha, Fern, and Louisa, symbolizes a sexuality longed for by the nameless male narrator. But whereas Toomer's Georgia women seem to have been repressed because no men can respond adequately to their vitality, Avey is a figure of bovine indolence who cannot herself respond to anything. When the narrator holds her tightly as they dance, she is "way away." When he gives her a burning kiss, she holds him in her lap like a child. Later, as he responds to the "soft dusk sky of Washington" where "the wind is from the South" and soil from his "homeland falls like a fertile shower upon the lean streets of the city," the narrator talks, sings, and recites his hopes to Avey (p. 85). This Wolfean attempt to express his inner life ends when he finds that she has fallen asleep. And like Wolfe's alter ego, Eugene Gant, Toomer's narrator finds no one who can share with him his buried longings, his half-expressed feelings.

The inability to communicate, which is articulated in "Avey" and was demonstrated in some of the earlier vignettes, becomes a major characteristic of the inadequacy of black urban life. Like a Eugene Gant hunting for a stone, leaf, or unfound door, some way to escape the isolation of self, Toomer's characters are either consciously or unconsciously locked within themselves. Their self-isolation, like the house that isolates Rhobert, is a further mark of their incomplete lives, their separation from other humans and the soil. And it is not words alone that fail them. In "Theater," John's "body is separate from the thoughts that pack his mind" (p. 92). He can only respond with "diluted passion" to the lovely Dorris who dances before him (p. 95). Instead of responding to the life in her, he is filled with his own shadowy dreams. The episode ends in mutual frustration as John and Dorris separate, each having missed the encounter which might have offered temporary escape and communication; in Wolfe's terms, they have missed a "bright moment of wonder, there on the magic island, where the world was quiet, believing all they said."

Dan Moore, protagonist of "Box Seat," is a tongue-tied would-be messiah come to heal his people. He perceives that Muriel and her schoolteacher friends, who not only accept and practice the values of white culture but transmit them to their students, are actually in prison. Their love and passion incarcerated at Muriel's boarding house, Dan and Muriel go separately to the theater to sit in seats that are described as "slots" in "bolted houses" where the people are the "bolted masses." In a surreal scene that suggests the later grotesqueries of Carson McCullers and Flannery O'Connor, two dwarfs fight on the stage. The winner then sings a sentimental song to Muriel and presents her with a rose he has kissed with his bloody lips. Although the audience applauds in their locklike seats, Muriel is filled with revulsion at the grotesque proceedings. Trapped, she can only accept the rose with a dainty, feminine gesture. Dan Moore, the prophet who sees the profanity of the performance, is paralyzed. Unable to act, he can only fantasize about the masculine role he should play, imagining himself a Samson pulling down the theater upon them all: "I am going to reach up and grab the girders of this building and pull them down. The crash will be a signal. Hid by the smoke and dust Dan Moore will rise. In his right hand will be a dynamo. In his left, a god's face that will flash white light from ebony. I'll grab a girder and swing it like a walking stick. Lightning will flash" (pp. 126–27). Such fantasies, of course, are of no value in a world of bolted lives and locked imaginations. Instead of subduing the world with light flashing from a god's face, Dan is himself subdued by a mirror flashed by the dwarf. The episode ends with Dan shouting "JESUS WAS ONCE A LEPER!" as he forces his way out of the theater. Such a comment is of no more pragmatic help than Dan's fantasies are. But it serves superbly as a judgment. In a world gone mad, the very Son of God becomes a polluted leper. Even the sacred is profane. Dan sees all of this, and with the rage of one of Flannery O'Connor's prophets, shouts it to an uncomprehending multitude, before he walks into the night, caught in his empty vision.

Toomer concludes part two of *Cane* with "Bona and Paul," an autobiographical vignette that depicts the racial, regional, and personal identity of an educated, sensitive man of mixed blood. Paul Johnson is a university student training to be a teacher; that is, he is learning to "give precision to the movements of sick people who all their lives have been drilling" (p. 134). Pursued by Bona Hale, a white student, Paul is pulled in so many ways that he is almost paralyzed. On the one hand, he remembers his ancestral past and the sun shining in a "pine-matted hillock in Georgia" where a "Negress chants a lullaby beneath the mate-eyes of a southern planter" (pp. 137–38). On the other hand, he is acutely conscious of his role as a student in Chicago. He sees that Bona is attracted to him, but he cannot decide whether she loves him as she says or is merely fascinated with his exotic appearance. He feels himself apart from the white people around him, who see "not attractiveness in his dark skin, but difference." On the dance floor Bona and Paul respond physically to each other and start to leave for what promises to be a splendid and beautiful moment. But when Paul stops to address the Negro doorman as "brother" and to tell him that something beautiful is going to happen, Bona disappears. Apparently, so long as Paul's racial identity is undefined, Bona is attracted to his "difference." But once he finally commits himself to her and makes the gesture that also identifies him racially with the black doorman, the mystery is over, and to Bona he is no longer a man, however exotic; he is merely a "nigger."

The ambiguities of identity, the poetic lyricism, the Gothic grotesqueries, the agrarian and regional longings, the isolation and frustration of an educated outsider, the paralysis and ineffectuality, indeed all of the major concerns of parts one and two of *Cane* come into focus in "Kabnis," the final section of Toomer's work. Ralph Kabnis is in his cabin bed in Georgia where "night winds are vagrant poets, whispering." Like Toomer, Kabnis is a dreamer come to teach in the South. Just like Wolfe's Eugene Gant, whose idealized self far transcends the reality of this existence, and George Webber, who wants to capture "a fragment of the truth about the life he knew and make it known and felt by others," so also Ralph Kabnis wants the ideal self of which he dreams to "become the face of the South." He wants his lips to sing of the South's soul. Gant and Webber return to the reality of drunken fathers, stingy mothers, and insensitive relatives. Kabnis returns to the reality of the rats of poverty and the dirt of slave-fields. Kabnis is torn between the very real beauty of nature that surrounds him and his awareness of the ugliness of the hog pen, the chicken yard, and the stinking outhouse amid which the black man lives. The resulting tension is analogous to the love and hatred toward the South expressed by Faulkner's Quentin Compson. Rather than shouting "I don't hate it! I don't hate it!" as Quentin does to his Harvard roommate, Kabnis asks himself, "Whats beauty anyway but ugliness if it hurts you?" and thinks of the "loneliness, dumbness, awful, intangible oppression" that "is enough to drive a man insane" (p. 162).

The native blacks respond to the life they find in several ways. Some are at peace because, unlike Kabnis, they do not intellectualize. They are oblivious to life's pain and ugliness. "They sing. They love. They sleep" (p. 164). In short, they are black noble savages close to the agrarian soil. Others see what the world is like and play

along, so they can exploit their fellow man. This group is represented by Mr. Hanby, a black school superintendent upon whom
Ralph Ellison might well have modeled his college president Mr.
Bledsoe. Hanby knows that to get along, he must play along with
the white power structure. He sees his job as proving "to the world
that the Negro race can be just like any other race" (p. 186). In
short, Hanby is one of those who press Rhobert's house upon his
head. Still others perceive reality but are neither paralyzed nor cor-
rupted. This group is represented by Lewis, a black who is not only
sensitive and perceptive, but active and vigorous. "His mouth and
eyes suggest purpose guided by an adequate intelligence. He is
what a stronger Kabnis [or Toomer] might have been" (p. 189).
Lewis embodies almost everything that Toomer's several protago-
nists/narrators want to be. It is to Lewis rather than to Kabnis that
the adolescent Carrie Kate is attracted. The implication is that
whereas Lewis can act and feel and be, Kabnis is as sterile and pas-
sive as the "mules tethered to odd trees and posts [which] blink
dumbly at him." Both Kabnis and the mules "seem burdened with
an impotent pain" (p. 205). When Lewis and Kabnis confront an an-
cient blind black preacher, Lewis can accept him as the "symbol,
flesh, and spirit of the past" (p. 217). Like Warren's Jack Burden before he has learned that he can only have the future if he can accept
the past, Kabnis denies the validity of his racial past as embodied in
the old preacher, and affirms a white past that refuses to accept him.
"An besides, he aint my past. My ancestors were Southern blue-
bloods" (p. 217). Kabnis is a kind of obverse Joe Christmas. Unlike
Christmas, who strikes back in pride and rage at a society that
forces him to be a nigger whether he is black or not (and who, after
killing Joanna Burden, finally deliberately chooses to put on the
black man's identity as well as his brogans), Kabnis denies the life-
giving roots he recognizes in the Negro peasant and that are affirmed by Lewis, to embrace a white heritage that even if it could
be his is of no value to him. Unlike Faulkner's Lucas Beauchamp,
who defines his manhood through constant warfare within and
against both his white and his black tradition, Kabnis loses his manhood because he refuses to face, straightforwardly and honestly, the
past that has made him. This refusal cuts Kabnis off not only from
his racial past but from life. As Lewis tells him: "Master; slave. Soil;

and the overarching heavens. Dusk; dawn. They fight and bastard-
ize you. The sun tint of your cheeks, flame of the great season's mul-
ticolored leaves, tarnished, burned. Split, shredded: easily burned.
No use" (p. 218). And as Kabnis gazes at the lovely Stella, she tells
him, "I aint got nothing f y mister. Taint no use t look at me"
(p. 218). While Lewis acts, then, Kabnis dreams and talks. Instead of listening to Father John, the blind old ex-slave and seer, as a part of
his past, Kabnis talks loudly and almost incoherently. When oracles
like Father John condemn the white man for making the "Bible lie,"
that is, for perverting the moral order of the universe, Kabnis first
chides him contemptuously and then crumples, ashamed and ex-
hausted, before the faith and simple acceptance of themselves expressed by the other blacks.

The romantically lyrical impulse is recurrently present in the
work of black and white southern novelists. It is in the work of
James Weldon Johnson, whose *Autobiography of an Ex-Coloured
Man* contains images later used in the verse sermons published in
God's Trombones. It is in the work of the failed-poet Faulkner, who
in *The Hamlet* (1931), for example, includes lyrical passages such as
"the motionless fronds of water-heavy grasses stooping into the mist
. . . fixed curves, along each parabola of which the marching drops
held in minute magnification the dawn's rosy miniatures, smelling
and even tasting the rich, slow, warm barn-reek milk-reek, the
flowing immemorial female."[9] It is in the work of Pulitzer Prize–
winning poet and novelist Robert Penn Warren, whose control of
southern rhetoric evokes sensuous responses in his prose as well as
in his verse. It is in the prose poems of Thomas Wolfe, whose char-

Throughout *Cane*, Toomer intersperses his vignettes with bits of
lyric verse. Almost all of these are poems celebrating southern
women, life, and soil. I have spent little time describing these
pieces, because characteristically they repetitiously describe a
woman or a setting in nature while attempting to evoke a mood. But
in considering Toomer as a southern writer, they are important for
two reasons: first, they align him with those southern novelists,
black and white, who also wrote either poetry or poetic prose; second, Toomer's poems repeatedly celebrate aspects of southern life
and nature.

acters grope "for the doorless land of faery" and wander through nights "brightly pricked with cool and tender stars" into "a cool bowl of lilac darkness, filled with fresh orchard scents."[10] This lyric celebration of life and land, so frequently present in southern fiction, is seen again and again in *Cane*.

> Wind is in the corn. Come along.
> Worn leaves swaying, rusty with talk,
> Scratching choruses above the guinea's squawk
> Wind is in the corn. Come along. (p. 18)

or

> Pour O Pour that parting soul in song,
> O pour it in the sawdust glow of night,
> Into the velvet pine-smoke air to-night,
> And let the valley carry it along
> And let the valley carry it along. (p. 21)

or

> Thunder blossoms gorgeously above our heads,
> Great, hollow, bell-like flowers,
> Rumbling in the wind,
> Stretching clappers to strike our ears . . .
> Full-lipped flowers
> Bitten by the sun
> Bleeding rain
> Dripping rain like golden honey—
> And the sweet earth flying from the thunder. (p. 90)

The Southerner's lyrical impulse is, in my judgment, a part of his response to an oral tradition of oratory and rhetoric. This tradition is seen in both the white and black southerner's religious and political experience. So strong is the tradition that it would be surprising indeed if it were not reflected in the literature of the region. Jean Toomer comes out of this tradition as did James Weldon Johnson before him, as did Faulkner, Wolfe, Warren, and Ellison after him. The lyricism is further evidence that Toomer is a southern as well as black writer.

The search for identity, the lyrical voice, the romantic agrarian vision, the Gothicism and grotesquerie, the attempted escape from isolation, the unreachable earth mother—all of these are the stock-in-trade of those writers whose works make up the southern fictional canon: Sims, Poe, Twain, Page, Faulkner, Wolfe, Warren, Capote, O'Connor, McCullers. And Toomer's work contained all of these elements before they appeared in the novels written by most of the writers just mentioned. They were all—black and white—responding to common parts of their southern cultural heritage.

Finally, the fact that *Cane* possesses so many recognizably southern literary characteristics while predating almost every modern southern novel of any stature is persuasive evidence that Toomer is part of a literary tradition that at its best unites so many as southerners rather than dividing them along racial lines.

V

A Clear Case
Richard Wright, 1908–1960

"Dick was a small-town boy—a small-town *Mississippi*
boy—all of his days. The hog maw and the collard
greens."   —Saunders Redding,
             "Reflections on Richard Wright"

"As a product of the South, Wright represented that
rare thing we sometimes call a clear case."
             —Arna Bontemps,
             "Reflections on Richard Wright"

Whatever ambiguity of regional
identity was embodied in the life of Jean Toomer, certainly little existed in that of Richard Wright. He was, in the words of Arna Bontemps, a southerner: "His deepest roots were in the folk culture of
the bottom—not *deep* but *bottom* —South. The lore of that milieu
was such an intimate part of his background he sometimes treated it
as if it had all originated in his own family."[1] And as Edward Margolies has rightly observed: "It is impossible to overestimate the
importance of these Southern years, for not only did they provide
Wright with the subject matter of many of his works, but they suggested to him all of his major themes, regardless of whether he was
writing about the urban proletariat in Chicago or the nationalist up-
heavals on the west coast of Africa."[2]

Born 4 September 1908 in Natchez, Mississippi, Wright was the
son of a sharecropper father who abandoned his family when Richard was six, and a schoolteacher mother who had sustained a crip-
pling paralytic stroke by the time he was ten.[3] Virtually destitute,

Richard and his family lived variously in Memphis, Tennessee; West Helena, Arkansas; and Jackson, Mississippi. At sixteen, with hardly more than four years of formal education, Richard finished the ninth grade as class valedictorian. During the same year, 1925, he moved from Jackson to Memphis, where he found work and saved his money. In 1927 he was able to move his mother, brother, and a maternal aunt to Chicago, where he worked as a postal clerk until the beginning of the Depression. By 1931 he was involved with the Federal Negro Theatre and the Illinois Writers Project under the auspices of the WPA.

During his stay in Memphis and later in Chicago, Wright educated himself through extensive if unsystematic reading at the public library. In 1932 he joined the Communist Party, an organization to which he gave himself unstintingly until 1944. Between 1932 and 1937 Wright wrote many poems, short stories, and essays, as well as being the Harlem editor of *The Daily Worker.* Four of his stories were published together as the prizewinning *Uncle Tom's Children* in 1938; in 1940 a fifth story was added. All depict southern blacks caught up in the irrational cruelty and violent injustice of southern racism.

Awarded a Guggenheim Fellowship in 1939, Wright completed *Native Son,* the work upon which more than any other his reputation rests. A Book-of-the-Month Club Selection, *Native Son* (1940) secured both Wright's fame and his financial well-being. It also won for him the Spingarn Medal, the NAACP's highest award for achievement by a Negro. In 1939 Wright married the white Rose Dhima Meadman, whom he divorced in 1941 to marry the white Ellen Poplar. He had two daughters by Poplar. In 1944 he left the Communist Party, an action he explained in "I Tried to Be a Communist," an extended essay written originally for the *Atlantic Monthly* but perhaps better known as a section of *The God That Failed.*[4] In 1944 he also published "The Man Who Lived Underground," a minor masterpiece employing as its basic metaphor the black man's subterranean existence, a metaphor developed even more artistically by Ralph Ellison in *Invisible Man.* In 1945 the autobiographical *Black Boy: A Record of Childhood and Youth* became Wright's second Book-of-the-Month Club Selection. In it he traces his life from his earliest recollections until he leaves the

South for Chicago at age nineteen. In 1947 Wright left the United States and settled in Paris. Active in the cultural life of postwar France, Wright was strongly influenced by the philosophical attitudes of Sartre, Camus, and other French intellectuals. *The Outsider*, published in 1953, reflects this influence.

Wright devoted his last years at least as much to international conferences, lecturing, essay writing, and travel as to creating fiction. His last complete novels, *Savage Holiday* and *The Long Dream*, were not well received by either his publishers or his public. On 28 November 1960 Richard Wright died of a heart attack in Paris. He was fifty-two.

Although Wright left the South before he was twenty (and America before he was forty), the South never left him, as he acknowledges at the end of *Black Boy*: "I was not leaving the South to forget the South, but so that some day I might understand it, might come to know what its rigors had done to me, to its children. . . . Yet, deep down, I knew that I could never really leave the South, for my feelings had already been formed by the South, for there had been slowly instilled into my personality and consciousness, black though I was, the culture of the South."[5] According to Saunders Redding, even as an expatriate he owned "a farm just outside Paris, and he bought that farm for one reason. He wanted to grow collard greens. He was quite frank about this. Raise some pigs and grow collard greens, because he had been brought up in the South on hog jowl and collard greens and he missed them in Paris."[6] Furthermore, critical judgment is nearly unanimous that Wright's best work—the stories in *Uncle Tom's Children*, the novel *Native Son*, and the autobiographical *Black Boy*—consists of material drawn from recollections of his Mississippi boyhood. And it is that material I wish to examine in this consideration of Richard Wright's relationship to a southern literary tradition.

Look Homeward, Black Boy

"A Record of Childhood and Youth," *Black Boy* belongs to the tradition of the literary autobiography. Ralph Ellison correctly observed that "in its use of fictional techniques, its concern with criminality (sin) and the artistic sensibility, and in its author's judgment and rejection of the narrow world of his origin, it recalls Joyce's rejection of Dublin in *A Portrait of the Artist*."[7] Although Ellison does not say so, *Black Boy* also recalls Thomas Wolfe's novelistic self-portrait in all his novels, and for exactly the same reasons. Wright, Joyce, and Wolfe combine autobiography with fiction to embody their moral visions, obsessively to reject the narrow world of their origin, and to draw their artistic self-portraits. Indeed, it is the fundamental similarity of subject matter, vision of human life, even, unlikely as one might think, the artistic devices used by Wolfe, especially in *Look Homeward, Angel* and by Wright in *Black Boy*, that despite their many differences unite Wolfe and Wright as southern writers.[8]

The story told in *Black Boy* (1945) closely parallels that told in *Look Homeward, Angel* (1929). Each begins with a protagonist's earliest recollections, establishes his essential estrangement from his family, traces his education—his rites of passage into manhood—and concludes with his train trip to the North, where he will become a writer. Early in *Black Boy* other obvious parallels appear. Wolfe's novel begins with a note to the reader acknowledging that "the author has written of experience which is now far and lost, but which was once part of the fabric of his life." Wright announces that he is transcribing a "record of childhood and youth." On the first page of his first chapter, Wolfe proclaims: "Each of us is all the sums he has not counted: subtract us into nakedness and night again, and you shall see begin in Crete four thousand years ago the love that ended yesterday in Texas. . . . Each moment is the fruit of forty thousand years. The minute-winning days, like flies, buzz home to death, and every moment is a window on all time. This is a moment."[9]

Only a few pages into *Black Boy* Wright tells us: "Each event spoke with a cryptic tongue. And the moments of living slowly revealed their coded meaning. There was the wonder I felt when I first saw a brace of mountainlike, spotted, black-and-white horses clopping down a dusty road through clouds of powdered clay" (p. 14). Not only is Wright's emphasis on the value of each moment to understanding our lives the same as Wolfe's, but like Wolfe he almost palpably evokes those moments through poetic images and incremental repetition. Although there are many instances throughout his novels where Wolfe conveys what it is to be alive through a protagonist's response to a litany of nature images, his account of the twelve-year-old Monk Webber's response when he looks at the world of his childhood is typical. It also strongly suggests Wright's account of Richard's attempt to understand the coded meaning of specific moments. Wolfe:

It is the place of the Springtime orchards, the loamy, dew-wet morning gardens, the peach, cherry, apple blossoms, drifting to the ground at morning in the month of April, the pungent, fragrant, maddening savor of the breakfast smells. It is the place of roses, lilies, and nasturtiums, the vine-covered porches of the houses, the strange, delicious smell of the ripening grapes in August, and the voices—near, strange, haunting, lonely, most familiar—of the people sitting on their porches in the Summer darkness, the voices of the lost people in the darkness as they say good-night. Then boys will hear a screen door slam, the earth grow silent with the vast and brooding ululation of the night, and finally the approach, the grinding screech, the brief halt, the receding loneliness and absence of the last street car going around the corner of the hill, and will wait there in the darkness filled with strangeness, thinking, "I was born here, there's my father, this is I!"

It is the world of the sun-warm, time-far clucking of the sensual hens in the forenoon strangeness of the spell of time, and the coarse, sweet coolness of Crane's cow along the alleyway; and it is the place of the ice-tongs ringing in the streets, the ice saw droning through the dripping blocks, the sweating negroes, and the pungent, musty, and exotic odors of the grocery wagons, the grocery box piled high with new provisions. It is the place of the forenoon housewives with their shapeless gingham dresses, bare legs, slippers, turbaned heads, bare, bony, labor-toughened hands and arms and elbows, and the fresh, clean, humid smell of houses airing in the morning. It is the place of the heavy midday dinners, the smells of roasts of beef, corn on the cob, the deep-hued savor of the big string beans, cooking morning long into the sweet amity and unction of the fat-streaked pork; and above it all is the clean, hungry, humid smell of the streaming freshness of the turnip greens at noon.

It is the world of magic April and October; world of the first green and the smell of blossoms; world of the bedded oak leaves and the smell of smoke in Autumn, and men in shirt-sleeves working in their yards in red waning light of old October as boys pass by them going home from school. It is the world of the Summer nights, world of the dream-strange nights of August, the great moons and the tolling bells; world of the Winter nights, the howling winds, and the fire-full chimney throats—world of the ash of time and silence while the piled coals flare and crumble, world of the waiting, waiting, waiting—for the world of joy, the longed-for face, the hoped-for step, the unbelieved-in magic of the Spring again.[10]

Wright:

There was the delight I caught in seeing long straight rows of red and green vegetables stretching away in the sun to the horizon.

There was the faint, cool kiss of sensuality when dew came on to my cheeks and shins as I ran down the wet green garden paths in the early morning.

There was the vague sense of the infinite as I looked down upon the yellow, dreaming waters of the Mississippi River from the verdant bluffs of Natchez.

There were the echoes of nostalgia I heard in the crying strings of wild geese winging south against a bleak, autumn sky.

There was the tantalizing melancholy in the tingling scent of burning hickory wood.

There was the teasing and impossible desire to imitate the petty pride of sparrows wallowing and flouncing in the red dust of country roads.

There was the yearning for identification loosed in me by the sight of a solitary ant carrying a burden upon a mysterious journey.

There was the disdain that filled me as I tortured a delicate, blue-pink crawfish that huddled fearfully in the mudsill of a rusty tin can.

There was the aching glory in masses of clouds burning gold and purple from an invisible sun.

There was the liquid alarm I saw in the blood-red glare of the sun's afterglow mirrored in the squared panes of whitewashed frame houses.

There was the languor I felt when I heard green leaves rustling with a rainlike sound.

There was the incomprehensible secret embodied in a whitish toadstool hiding in the dark shade of a rotting log.

There was the experience of feeling death without dying that came from watching a chicken leap about blindly after its neck had been snapped by a quick twist of my father's wrist.

There was the great joke that I felt God had played on cats and dogs by making them lap their milk and water with their tongues.

There was the thirst I had when I watched clear, sweet juice trickle from sugar cane being crushed.

There was the hot panic that welled up in my throat and swept through my blood when I first saw the lazy, limp coils of a blue-skinned snake sleeping in the sun.

There was the speechless astonishment of seeing a hog stabbed through the heart, dipped into boiling water, scraped, split open, gutted, and strung up gaping and bloody.

There was the love I had for the mute regality of tall, moss-clad oaks.

There was the hint of cosmic cruelty that I felt when I saw the curved timbers of a wooden shack that had been warped in the summer sun.

There was the saliva that formed in my mouth whenever I smelt clay dust potted with fresh rain.

There was the cloudy notion of hunger when I breathed the odor of new-cut, bleeding grass.

And there was the quiet terror that suffused my senses when vast hazes of gold washed earthward from star-heavy skies on silent nights. (pp. 14–15)

Not only does Wright suggest Wolfe's sense of the specific moment and intensify its meaning through evocative language and repetition, he also, like Wolfe, stresses the relationship between that moment and his protagonist's longing for a sense of identity. Late in his first chapter Wright seems deliberately to replicate attitudes Wolfe expresses in the famous prose poem which prefaces *Look Homeward, Angel*. Wolfe:

. . . a stone, a leaf, an unfound door; of a stone, a leaf, a door. And of all the forgotten faces.

Naked and alone we came into exile. In her dark womb we did not know our mother's face; from the prison of her flesh have we come into the unspeakable and incommunicable prison of this earth.

Which of us has known his brother? Which of us has looked into his father's heart? Which of us has not remained forever prison-pent? Which of us is not forever a stranger and alone?

O waste of loss, in the hot mazes, lost, among bright stars on this most weary unbright cinder, lost! Remembering speechlessly we seek the great forgotten language, the lost lane-end into heaven, a stone, a leaf, an unfound door. Where? When?

O lost, and by the wind grieved, ghost, come back again. (p. 1)

Instead of writing a poetic set piece, Wright incorporates a description of his sense of longing, of isolation, in an account of meeting his

father for the first time some twenty-five years after his father abandoned the family. Wright describes the scene in realistic detail, em-
phasizing his father's ragged overalls and the muddy hoe in his
gnarled, veined hands (recalling Wolfe's emphasis on W. O. Gant's
great hands in *Look Homeward, Angel*), then going on to say:

> Though I could see a shadow of my face in his face, though there
> was an echo of my voice in his voice, we were forever strangers,
> speaking a different language, living on vastly different planes of re-
> ality. . . . I was overwhelmed to realize that he could never under-
> stand me or the scalding experiences that had swept me beyond his
> life and into an area of living that he could never know. I stood be-
> fore him, poised, my mind aching as it embraced the simple naked-
> ness of his life, feeling how completely his soul was imprisoned by
> the slow flow of the seasons, by wind and rain and sun, how fas-
> tened were his memories to a crude and raw past, how chained
> were his actions and emotions to the direct, animalistic impulses of
> his withering body. (pp. 42–43)

Despite the differences in form, the sense of isolation and estrangement from one's closest relatives, those who have given us
life, dominates both passages. Furthermore, key words and phrases
are common to *Black Boy* and *Look Homeward, Angel*.

WOLFE: Which of us is not forever a stranger and alone.
WRIGHT: We were forever strangers.

WOLFE: Remembering speechlessly we seek the great forgotten
language.
WRIGHT: . . . speaking a different language, living on vastly different planes of reality.

WOLFE: O waste of loss, in the hot mazes.
WRIGHT: . . . the scalding experiences that had swept me beyond
his life.

WOLFE: Naked and alone we came into exile.
WRIGHT: . . . my mind aching as it embraced the simple nakedness
of his life.

WOLFE: From the prison of her flesh have we come into the unspeakable and incommunicable prison of this earth.
WRIGHT: . . . feeling how completely his soul was imprisoned by
the slow flow of the seasons, by wind and rain and sun.

Even so, the world of *Black Boy* apparently exists in a different universe from that of *Look Homeward, Angel.* Eugene Gant is white, Richard is black. Although the Gants were of modest means, Eugene did not know the grinding poverty young Richard endured. Although Eugene's father is a stonecutter, he is a middle-class man who loves Shakespeare, not an illiterate sharecropper. Although Eliza Gant is stingy and unduly concerned with acquiring property, she is a vital force, paralyzed in neither body nor spirit. And despite the separation of Eugene's father and mother, they are both very real presences in the life of the family; there is no sense of abandonment by the father. Certainly Eugene's education at the Altamont Fitting School, his entry into the state university at sixteen years of age, and his subsequent academic career can be no more than ironically parallel to Richard's ninth-grade valedictory at age sixteen. Most important, the oppressive racism Richard endures simply has no parallel of any kind in Eugene Gant's experience. What, then, constitutes the similarity between the world of young Richard and that of Eugene Gant? It is of course the similarity of the protagonists' responses to the experience of being alive. Both depict an existence that is estranged from that of others, "lonely at the core," and both test and affirm the worth of the self.

Like Wolfe (and Joyce), early in his autobiographical work Wright presents his first recollections of childhood. Unlike Eugene's innocent impressionistic views from the crib (and baby tuckoo's obsession with moocows), Richard's first memories are of guilt, terror, and violence: guilt for having set fire to his grandmother's house, terror at what the consequences to himself would be, and violence in the form of a mother's beating that left him senseless. The meanings in these moments are quite different from those in the early moments remembered by Eugene Gant. Eugene's earliest recollections show him his "unfathomable loneliness"; his inability to talk is emblematic of his life-long sense that "men [are] forever strangers to one another." His sense that "he heard a great bell ringing faintly, as it sounded undersea," suggests to him the lone ghost of himself he has lost by assuming physical life (p. 31). Yet for both the essential point is that the meaning is in the moments, in the experiences which are both the reality of our existences and the basis of our understanding.

What Richard learns is that he must either fight or be a victim. He learns this when his mother forces him to face the bullies who attempt to extort grocery money from him (pp. 24–25). When his father abandons the family, Richard learns that he cannot rely on this "law giver," this authority figure to provide for and protect him (pp. 21–22). He also begins to ask the question raised by so many southern novelists—"why does evil exist?" Why do some people have enough food and others do not? (p. 26). Why cannot the law courts see to it that his mother is treated justly by his father? (pp. 34–35). Why do the whites treat the blacks with such vicious hatred? If grandmother's skin is so white, why is she black? (p. 31). Unable to get answers even to his factual questions, much less the philosophical ones behind them, Richard learns not to trust anyone or anything (p. 37). Sensitive and headstrong, he finds himself continually embroiled in clashes with his older relatives. And as he turns increasingly to the world of the mind—of knowledge and of literature—he finds himself increasingly isolated from and rejected by his family. A roomer at the house whispers to him the story of Bluebeard and he learns—as does Eugene Gant—of the power of words to open "the gateway to a forbidden and enchanting land" (p. 49).

Both Eugene and Richard also use physical sensation as a means of escape. As a youth Eugene Gant escaped some of the meanness of his life—the quarrels between his drunken father and penurious mother, his sense of being forever isolated—by turning to specific physical responses.

Thus, pent in his dark soul, Eugene sat brooding on a fire-lit book, a stranger in a noisy inn. The gates of his life were closing him in from their knowledge, a vast aerial world of fantasy was erecting its fuming and insubstantial fabric. . . .

He had heard already the ringing of remote church bells over a countryside on Sunday night; he had listened to the earth steeped in the brooding of dark, and the million-noted little night things; and he had heard thus the far retreating wail of a whistle in a distant valley, and faint thunder on the rails; and he felt the infinite depth and width of the golden world in the brief deductions of a thousand multiplex and mixed mysterious odors and sensations, weaving, with a blinding interplay and aural explosions, one into the other. (pp. 68–69)

There follows an extended Wolfean catalogue of smells, sounds, sights, and feelings. Similarly, when Richard's unintentional insult to his grandmother results in rejection and punishment that seem incomprehensible to him, he too turns to his sensations:

The days and hours began to speak now with a clearer tongue. Each experience had a sharp meaning of its own.
There was the breathlessly anxious fun of chasing and catching flitting fireflies on drowsy summer nights.
There was the drenching hospitality in the pervading smell of sweet magnolias.
There was the aura of limitless freedom distilled from the rolling sweep of tall green grass swaying and glinting in the wind and sun.
There was the feeling of impersonal plenty when I saw a boll of cotton whose cup had split over and straggled its white fleece toward the earth.
There was the pitying chuckle that bubbled in my throat when I watched a fat duck waddle across the back yard.
There was the suspense I felt when I heard the taut, sharp song of a yellow-black bee hovering nervously but patiently above the white rose. . . .
There was the puckerly taste that almost made me cry when I ate my first half-ripe persimmon.
There was the greedy joy in the tangy taste of wild hickory nuts.
There was the dry hot summer morning when I scratched my bare arms on briers while picking blackberries and came home with fingers and lips stained black with sweet berry juice.
There was the relish of eating my first fried fish sandwich, nibbling at it slowly and hoping that I would never eat it up.
There was the all-night ache in my stomach after I had climbed a neighbor's tree and eaten stolen, unripe peaches.
There was the morning when I thought I would fall dead from fear after I had stepped with my bare feet upon a bright little green garden snake.
And there were the long, slow, drowsy days and nights of drizzling rain. (pp. 53–55)

Wright's explanation of Richard's escape into the faraway country of his imagination in the face of racial and family oppression is certainly comparable to Wolfe's account of Eugene's escape into the world of books and learning. Wright:

Up or down the wet or dusty streets, indoors or out, the days and nights began to spell out magic possibilities. . . .
Anything seemed possible, likely, feasible, because I wanted everything to be possible. . . . Because I had no power to make things happen outside of me in the objective world, I made things happen within. Because my environment was bare and bleak, I endowed it with unlimited potentialities, redeemed it for the sake of my own hungry and cloudy yearning. (pp. 81–83)

Wolfe:

Eugene spent the next few years of his life in Leonard's school. Against the bleak horror of Dixieland, against the dark road of pain and death down which the great limbs of Gant had already begun to slope, against all the loneliness and imprisonment of his own life which had gnawed him like hunger, these years at Leonard's bloomed like golden apples. (p. 180).

And Eugene also escapes into his daydreams of himself as the "Dixie Ghost," the hero of romantic films and novels: "He was those heroes whom he admired, and the victor, in beauty, nobility, and sterling worth, over those whom he despised because they always triumphed and were forever good and pretty and beloved of women" (p. 227).

Richard's life amid wracking poverty and racial bigotry is not the same as Eugene's life amid family squabbles in a boarding house that caters to prostitutes. The result for both lives, however, is a turning inward, a sense of isolation and estrangement, and an escape into a world of sensations, of the imagination, of words, of reading.

Both Wright and Wolfe use family tragedies to symbolize the essential meaninglessness of human life. In *Black Boy* a mother's paralysis and suffering symbolize all the poverty, ignorance, helplessness, hunger-ridden days and hours, restless moving, futile seeking, fear, dread, meaningless pain, and endless suffering Richard has known. Richard comes to the "conviction that the meaning of living came only when one was struggling to wring a meaning out of meaningless suffering" (p. 112). In *Look Homeward, Angel* the death of one of her sons from typhoid brings to

Eliza Gant a consciousness of "the inexorable tides of Necessity" and a feeling of sorrow "for all who had lived, were living, or would live, fanning with their prayers the useless altar flames, suppliant with their hopes to an unwitting spirit, casting the tiny rockets of their belief against remote eternity, and hoping for grace, guidance, and delivery upon the spinning and forgotten cinder of this earth. O lost" (p. 49).

Just as Wright's and Wolfe's visions of life's ultimate meaninglessness coincide, so also do their visions of what gives life such limited value as it has. Richard retains a love of everything that keeps alive in him the enthralling sense of wonder and awe in the face of the drama of human feeling which is hidden by the external drama of life" (p. 112). Wolfe's "Story of the Buried Life" celebrates these moments of wonder which allow us to forget life's pain and conflict and to escape its isolation (pp. 376–80). And whereas Wright finds his strength in a tolerant skepticism allowing him both to sympathize with and criticize his fellow men, while Wolfe's comes from a romantic imagination allowing him occasionally to transcend human evils, both affirm an essential sense of awe and wonder at the very experience of being alive. Although Wolfe would have expressed it differently, he would have understood Wright's inability to accept his mother's Christianity: "My faith, such as it was, was welded to the common realities of life, anchored in the sensations of my body and in what my mind could grasp, and nothing could ever shake this faith, and surely not my fear of an invisible power" (p. 127). Almost every word Wolfe wrote was an attempt to test the limits of language, to force it to accomplish what, in Wright's words, finally could not be done: ". . . and I knew more than she thought I knew about the meaning of religion, the hunger of the human heart for that which is not and can never be, the thirst of the human spirit to conquer and transcend the implacable limitations of human life" (pp. 131–32).

Interestingly enough, the life of the imagination which sustained Richard and Eugene in their estrangement also served to isolate them further from family and peers. As a child Richard hears the story of Bluebeard, and his grandmother rages that such fiction is the child of the devil. As a child young Richard reads a story he has written to a woman in the neighborhood and sees her bafflement and astonishment. "God only knows what she thought. My environment contained nothing more alien than writing or the desire to express one's self in writing" (p. 133). When he sells papers so that he can read the cheap pulp tales they contain, he unknowingly isolates himself further from the black community, because the paper itself is anti-Negro (pp. 142–46). And as he looks at his schoolmates, his peers, he sees himself doomed to being different: "Again and again I vowed that someday I would end this hunger of mine, this apartness, this eternal difference; and I did not suspect that I would never get intimately into their lives, that I was doomed to live with them but not of them, that I had my own strange and separate road, a road which in later years would make them wonder how I had come to tread it" (p. 140). When as a bored, unmotivated eighth grader he writes a story that a local Negro paper prints, his classmates are more baffled than ever. "They looked at me with new eyes, and a distance, a suspiciousness came between us" (p. 184). With no encouragement from teachers, family, or friends, Richard dreams of "going north and writing books, novels" (p. 186). Louis D. Rubin's description of the white southern writer's relationship to his family and the white community fits Richard's relationship to his family and community almost exactly:

So the Southerner engaged in becoming a writer departed again—whether he departed literally or figuratively does not matter. . . . But he was not a part of the community any longer; not really, not even if he pretended to himself that he was. His standards were different, his attitudes toward the common Southern experience were different. He may have become very "Southern"—but in a quite self-conscious way, as if playing a game with himself. For one cannot really be self-consciously Southern. . . . One cannot be mentally detached from the Southern community while physically a part of it, and be fully a member of that community. The essence of membership in the old Southern community was the sense of belonging, of being able to define one's place, one's attitude, one's identity as a man, through one's role in that community's life. When the community ceased to provide that anchor and definition, then in an important sense it no longer existed.[11]

Again, Eugene Gant's experience is both different and similar. It was on the basis of an impromptu essay he wrote in school that he was selected to be a student in the Altamont Fitting School. And the teacher who so influenced his life encouraged him to read, to write, to study. But his family, including, ironically, his father, did not understand the life of the mind, of the imagination. Rather, for them the value of an education was primarily material, and in order to secure the funds to attend Harvard for postgraduate work, Eugene (like Wolfe himself) had to sign a statement renouncing any other claims he might have to his father's estate. In addition, when Thomas Wolfe lived that experience, he had to mislead his family into believing that he intended to study journalism—practical writing that produced an income—rather than creative writing.

At eighteen Richard says goodbye to his mother and leaves for Memphis on money he has skimmed from the receipts at a movie house where he took tickets. He soon finds work, and with the help of a Catholic Yankee expatriate, begins to read voluminously at the library: Anderson, Masters, Mencken, Dreiser, and Lewis. Through reading he discovers some of the feelings and experiences he has been denied by his life as a southern black. His physical hunger that had early become a hunger to be accepted by his peers now becomes a new hunger fully to live and to know and to be (p. 274). It is the same hunger to which Wolfe alludes in the subtitle to *Of Time and the River: A Legend of Man's Hunger in His Youth.* And Wolfe/Eugene's response to this hunger is the same as Wright/Richard's: "He read insanely, by the hundreds, the thousands, the ten thousands. . . . He simply wanted to know about everything on earth; he wanted to devour the earth, and it drove him mad when he saw that he could not do this."[12]

Black Boy ends with the nineteen-year-old Richard aboard a northbound train preparing to move his family to Chicago. As he leaves Memphis he recalls the oppression, the brutality, the dehumanizing qualities of the southern life he is escaping. Even so, he acknowledges his identity as a southerner:

I was not leaving the South to forget the South, but so that some day I might understand it, might come to know what its rigors had done to me, to its children. I fled so that the numbness of my defensive living might thaw out and let me feel the pain—years later and far away—of what living in the South had meant.
Yet, deep down, I knew that I could never really leave the South, for my feelings had already been formed by the South, for there had

been slowly instilled into my personality and consciousness, black though I was, the culture of the South. So, in leaving, I was taking a part of the South to transplant in alien soil, to see if it could grow differently, if it could drink of new and cool rains, bend in strange winds, respond to the warmth of other suns, and, perhaps, to bloom. . . . And if that miracle ever happened, then I would know that there was yet hope in that southern swamp of despair and violence, that light could emerge even out of the blackest of the southern night. I would know that the South too could overcome its fear, its hate, its cowardice, its heritage of guilt and blood, its burden of anxiety and compulsive cruelty. (pp. 284–285)

Look Homeward, Angel ends and *Of Time and the River* begins with a twenty-year-old Eugene at the train station preparing to go to Harvard. Although the effect of the South on the departing Eugene is not specifically depicted at this time in either work, earlier in *Look Homeward, Angel* feelings of rejection and frustration similar to Richard's were described as something remembered from the North:

Years later, when he could no longer think of the barren spiritual wilderness, the hostile and murderous entrenchment against all new life—when their cheap mythology, their legend of the charm of their manner, the aristocratic culture of their lives, the quaint sweetness of their drawl, made him writhe—when he could think of no return to their life and its swarming superstition without weariness and horror, so great was his fear of the legend, his fear of their antagonism, that he still pretended the most fanatic devotion to them, excusing his Northern residence on grounds of necessity rather than desire. (p. 127)

Like Faulkner's Quentin Compson, who could not tell his Harvard roommate about the South without hating and loving both it and a part of himself, Wolfe and Wright describe their own mixed feelings about the South, and, like Quentin, only half understand the South's effect upon themselves and their own attitude toward it.

What is one to make of all of these parallel statements about the meaning of moments, the comparable evocative lists, the echoing phrases of estrangement? What conclusions are we to draw from the parallel escapes from reality into the life of language, books, and the imagination? The use of family suffering as an emblem of life's ultimate meaninglessness? The paradoxical emphasis on the wonder and awe of being alive? The great spiritual hunger that both Richard and Eugene satisfy through compulsive reading? The flight North so that both can become writers? Beyond doubt, these parallels are different in kind as well as in degree from those similarities of attitude and theme which unite the works of Chesnutt, Johnson, and Toomer with those of their white southern colleagues. Did Wright deliberately create them to underscore the relationship he saw between himself and Wolfe, a relationship that far transcends differences of race? I think that he did. Born within the same decade, both were southerners who overcame many of the limits of family and social environment. Both left the South to become successful novelists. Both saw the meaning of life embodied in specific moments, in sensations reachable by the imaginative mind. But perhaps as much as anything else, Wright saw in Wolfe an estrangement from the very South that produced him which was comparable to his own. Wright's attitude toward the South is, at least, little different from George Webber's in *You Can't Go Home Again*: "For he was a Southerner, and he knew that there was something wounded in the South. He knew that there was something twisted, dark, and full of pain which Southerners have known with all their lives—something rooted in their souls beyond all contradiction, about which no one had dared to write, of which no one had ever spoken."[13] Like Wolfe, Wright knew he could not go home again. Like Wright, Wolfe knew that he could never leave the South that had formed him. To a degree, each saw the South as a dark satanic angel when he looked homeward.

Native Southerner

If the evidence suggesting that Richard Wright both read and responded to Thomas Wolfe must be inferred, his knowledge of William Faulkner and the other major southern writers is explicitly evident. By 1935–36 he was reading Faulkner as one of the avant-garde writers of the period, and counted *The Sound and the Fury* (along with *Moby Dick* and *Ulysses*) among his favorite novels.[14] In an interview entitled "L'Homme du Sud," given on the occasion of Faulkner's receiving the Nobel Prize, Wright pronounced his judgment: "His hateful statements of racism will be forgotten, but the gallery of Faulkner's characters will live as long as men feel the need to know themselves, as long as troubled spirits who need peace and an opportunity for reflection, seek refuges in those books which form the reservoir of the emotional experiences of a nation."[15] And Wright was in turn read by Faulkner. In 1945 Faulkner wrote to Wright: "I have just read *Black Boy*. . . . It needed to be said. . . . You said it well, as well as it could have been said in this form. Because I think you said it much better in *Native Son*. I hope you will keep on saying it, but I hope you will say it as an artist, as in *Native Son*."[16] Wright also knew well the works of other southern writers. In 1940 he wrote a highly favorable review of *The Heart Is a Lonely Hunter* for the *New Republic* in which he praised Carson McCullers (later to become a friend) as the first southern novelist to create black and white characters equally well. He quoted Twain in *The Long Dream* (1958), his last novel. And in January 1951 he "traced the literature of the South from Faulkner to Flannery O'Connor" in a lecture delivered in Genoa and Rome.[17]

Even so, the literary elements Wright shares with Faulkner and other white southern writers are more nearly of a kind with those traced in the works of Chesnutt, Johnson, and Toomer than they are with the direct allusions and paraphrases seen in *Black Boy*. Certainly the stories in *Uncle Tom's Children*, based on material from Wright's childhood memories of black Mississippi life, are much more nearly Wright's literary material than is *The Outsider*.[18] A similar statement about Faulkner's Yoknapatawpha materials as opposed, say, to *A Fable* would be as self-evidently true.

Aside from this general similarity there are specific qualities in Wright's work that suggest his literary relationship to Faulkner and other southern novelists. *Native Son* is particularly rife with such southern fictional elements as Gothic symbolism, violence, and the grotesque; the inverted Christ-figure; the conflict between free will and determinism; the protagonist's search for identity.

Native Son is the story of a few months in the life of Bigger Thomas, a twenty-year-old black described by the local prosecuting attorney as "just a scared colored boy from Mississippi."[19] As is typically the case with southern authors' protagonists, Bigger grew up in the writer's home town, Jackson, Mississippi. His portrait was drawn, as Wright explained in "How Bigger Was Born," from the examples of five young blacks he had known there (viii–xi). Like Wright's own broken family, Bigger's moved to Chicago during his teenage years to escape the oppression of life in the South. Unfortunately, Bigger Thomas has neither the will, the intelligence, nor the good fortune of Richard Wright. Instead of a new life, he finds death. He accidentally kills Mary Dalton, the daughter of the family that has hired him as a chauffeur, a family that wants to help him improve himself. After burning Mary's body in a furnace, Bigger attempts to shift suspicion from himself to Jan Erlone, Mary's Communist boy friend. Then, to extort money, he sends a ransom note to the family. When Mary's skeletal remains are found, Bigger flees with his girl friend Bessie, whom he soon murders because he believes her presence will cause him to be caught. Hunted down like an animal, Bigger is convicted of rape and murder, and is on his way to be executed as the novel ends.

Native Son opens in the one-bedroom Thomas apartment with the trapping and killing of a rat by Bigger—a symbolic foreshadowing of Bigger's own fate. (The episode is much more akin to Steinbeck's use of the overturned tortoise in *The Grapes of Wrath* than it is to the symbolism of a Faulkner or a Warren.) The dominant symbolic pattern of the novel, however, consists of a Gothic image of confused entrapment in a white world, populated by threatening freaks, that Bigger enters when he begins to live with and work for the rich Daltons. It is a Gothic world of white, just as the tomblike rooms of Faulkner's Emily Grierson and Rosa Coldfield are Gothic worlds of black. Like Capote's Joel Knox, in *Other Voices, Other Rooms* (1948), who escapes the frightening truth that he cannot function as a heterosexual male by fanciful visits to an imaginary room filled with imaginary voices, Bigger escapes the ugly reality of his ghetto life by entering the white dream world of the movies and by playing fantasy games in which he and his friend Gus are rich and white (pp. 17, 21, 33–35). And like Joel, to whom the reality of his being is symbolized by a world of houses sinking into swamps, by paralyzed fathers, transvestite cousins, and gnomelike blacks, the reality of the white world to Bigger is represented by a blind woman dressed in white and accompanied by a white cat, a woman who seems to him to be a ghost. It consists of people who talk in an incomprehensible language about "wise procedures," injecting him "into his new environment," and "using the analysis contained in the case record"; it is inhabited by a family whose behavior is totally inexplicable to him (pp. 48–55). Bigger is so disoriented that he does not know whether to enter the front door or the back (p. 45). He wants to escape this grotesque world by waving a hand and blotting out either the white man or himself (pp. 49–50). Unable to do either, and surrounded by the white kitchen walls of his strange new world, he feels a Kafkaesque guilt (pp. 51, 55–56). Wright insists on the Gothic quality the white world holds for Bigger. "Ghost-like, Mrs. Dalton moved noiselessly, . . . the big white cat following her" (pp. 189–90). Her face reminds him of a "dead man's face" (p. 61). When he rides between Mary Dalton and Jan Erlone, he sits between "two vast white looming walls" (p. 68). When Mrs. Dalton comes into her drunken daughter's room where Bigger is putting her to bed, an entrance which causes Bigger to smother Mary to prevent her from calling out, Mrs. Dalton seems like an "awesome white blur" and Bigger feels that he is "in the grip of a weird spell" (pp. 85–86).

If when Bigger enters the white world he enters a world of the southern Gothic, his attempt to escape the consequences of accidentally killing Mary Dalton is an exercise in the southern gruesome. Like a desperate Mink Snopes (*The Hamlet*, 1931) trying first to hide and then to move the decomposing body of Jack Houston after murdering him, Bigger exists in Poe's nightmarish world of desperate terror as he forces Mary's body into a trunk. Then, unable to get her wholly into the blazing furnace, he cuts off her head in a display of southern, if not patriotic, gore (pp. 81–91) reminiscent of Joe Christmas's assault on Joanna Burden. And as is the case in the work of such practitioners of the southern Gothic as McCullers, Capote, Faulkner, and O'Connor, Wright's Gothic serves as an emblem of his protagonist's spiritual and moral disorientation as he attempts to function in a world with which he is unequipped to deal. Bigger's violence suggests the horrible consequences of such spiritual disorientation.

Like all of the black southern writers considered in this study, and many of their white confreres, Wright focuses much of his attention on the question of his protagonist's sense of identity. Unlike

Chesnutt's John Walden and Janet Miller, Johnson's ex-coloured man, or Toomer's Toomer, Wright's Bigger Thomas is not concerned with defining his identity in terms of whether or not he is black. Bigger knows he is black. His question is, Am I human? His ostensible answer is no. Not only is his physical appearance different from the white norm, his behavior seems inexplicable in any rational terms. To his mother, Bigger's humanity means that he should play the traditional male role by getting a job, getting the family off relief, being a good Christian, and emulating Booker T. Washington (p. 12). Bigger rejects this role because he sees his mother and family suffering and helpless. Indeed, were he ever consciously to accept the role allotted him and his family, he would—like Chesnutt's Josh Green, Faulkner's Joe Christmas, or Styron's Will (in *The Confessions of Nat Turner*)—either kill himself or someone else (p. 14). "The rhythms of his life" become "indifference and violence" (p. 31). Bigger picks a fight with and humiliates his friend Gus to prevent, as Gus tells him, anyone from seeing that Bigger is afraid to rob a white man. The chance Mr. Dalton offers Bigger through work and education has no meaning to him; the abstract discussion by Jan and Mary of Negroes as humans, too, fills him with rage and a desire to destroy them and himself (pp. 56–57, 70). As a result, when he kills Mary, an act that since Cain has separated murderers from their fellow men, the paradoxical result for Bigger is not only isolation but a discovery of himself and a sense of identity. That is, because his own sense of life and humanity has been so completely denied up to this point, the act of murder creates a new life for him. His crime becomes the first thing he has ever had that no one could take away from him. "The hidden meaning of his life—a meaning which others did not see and which he had always tried to hide—had spilled out. . . . It was as though he had an obscure but deep debt to fulfill to himself in accepting the deed" (p. 101).

Bigger's conduct and his attitude toward it are comparable to that of Faulkner's Charles Etienne de Saint Valery Bon (*Absalom, Absalom!*, 1936) and Joe Christmas (*Light in August*, 1932). Both Bon and Christmas turn to violence as their means of combating the social roles assigned them because they must be black. Like Bigger, Bon seems to look for chances to pick fights. To show the absurdity

of his being classed a Negro and having to accept the consequent
social stigma, Bon marries the blackest, most apelike creature he
can find. Depending upon his mood, Joe Christmas gets into fights
with anyone who suggests that he is either black or white. And he
spends some sixteen years symbolically raping white women by first
seducing or paying them and then telling them he is a Negro. The
parallel between the behavior Faulkner describes and that depicted
by Wright goes beyond their both being forms of antisocial violence. Bigger is convicted of raping Mary Dalton. And even though
he did not actually do so, he accepts the symbolic validity of the
charge:

Had he raped her? Yes, he had raped her. Every time he felt as he
had felt that night, he had raped. But rape was not what one did to
women. Rape was what one felt when one's back was against a wall
and one had to strike out, whether one wanted to or not, to keep
the pack from killing one. He committed rape every time he looked
into a white face. He was a long, taut piece of rubber which a thousand white hands had stretched to the snapping point, and when he
snapped it was rape. But it was rape when he cried out in hate deep
in his heart as he felt the strain of living day by day. That, too, was
rape. (pp. 213–14)

Such a definition explains not only the meaning of Bigger's murderous act, but the meaning in both Bon's and Christmas's physical
violence and use of sex as symbolic assault. All are instinctive attempts to fight, to strike back against, to punish a system of racial
caste by injuring individuals against whom little or no personal ani-
mosity is felt because that person, especially a white woman, is
ruled to be untouchable by the black male. By having their protagonists consciously or unconsciously, actually or symbolically violate
this taboo, these two Mississippi writers display an almost identical
attitude toward and understanding of the conduct of Bon, Christmas, and Bigger Thomas. By having Percy Grimm yell "Now you'll
let white women alone, even in hell"[20] as he castrates a dying Joe
Christmas, and by having the prosecuting attorney argue at Bigger's
trial that "the central crime here is *rape*" (p. 377), Faulkner and
Wright show that those destructive representatives of a twisted justice not only see at one level the true nature of Joe's and Bigger's
crime, but understand its defiant meaning as well.

Another important similarity between Bigger Thomas and Joe Christmas is that both are inverted Christ figures. Joe's name and initials, his illegitimate birth, his cleansing of the Negro church, and his semi-sacrificial death all suggest a Christ parallel. His pride, his self-isolation from those like Byron Bunch who would share food with him, his rejection of the white man's religion and his defilement of his women are details which suggest that Christmas is, as a semihysterical woman at the Negro church says, "the devil! It's Satan himself" (p. 305).

Bigger's rejection of Christianity, like that of Christmas, begins early and continues throughout the novel. Indeed, he not only rejects the entreaties of a black preacher after he is arrested, he throws coffee in the face of a white priest who visits him after his conviction. Even so, anticipating O'Connor's Misfit, he wishes for "someone [who] had gone before and lived or suffered or died— made it so that it could be understood!" He longs, echoing the words of Jesus, "to lose himself . . . so he could find himself" (p. 226). Instead of discovering a Christ, however, in a sense he becomes one. When he is captured "two men stretched his arms out, as though about to crucify him" (p. 253). When he is carried back to the scene of the murder after the inquest, spittle splashes against his face and he sees a wooden cross burning across the street. Much like the church music in *Light in August*, which has "a quality stern and implacable . . . pleading, asking, for not love, not life, forbidding it to others, demanding in sonorous tones death as though death were the boon, like all Protestant music" (p. 347), the cross Bigger was given by the black preacher becomes a cross of hatred rather than love, "an evil and black charm which would surely bring him death now." After he throws the cross away "his body seemed a flaming cross," and like those who enter hell, he abandons all hope (pp. 313–15). Although both Bigger Thomas and Joe Christmas reject Christianity, indeed affirm a creed of rebellion, violence, and death that is antithetical to Christ's teachings, both become sacrificial scapegoats executed by the community or its self-appointed representative.[21]

There are other similarities. For Joe Christmas, memory knows before knowing remembers. That is, as an adult he does not consciously know the forces, experiences, episodes from his past which subconsciously operate in his present life. At the end of the novel, Bigger Thomas only dimly begins to perceive the forces that have caused him to feel guilt and fear all of his life. Joe Christmas feels that he can see himself being hunted into the abyss at last by white men trying to destroy him, when all he has ever wanted is peace (p. 313). When he is caught by Grimm, Joe seems to confirm an implicit death wish; he does not defend himself even though he has a loaded pistol. Throughout *Native Son*, Bigger sees himself as pursued, controlled, and isolated from life by the whites. He too wants only the peace that would come if he could "blot out" everything (p. 307). "An organic wish to cease to be, to stop living, seized him" (p. 319).

More than any other of Faulkner's major novels, *Light in August* suggests that man's free will is at best severely limited and at worst denied by social forces against which he is almost powerless. In his introduction to that novel, Cleanth Brooks suggests this attitude when he writes: "Faulkner could hardly have stressed more emphatically that Joe's status as 'nigger' is a state of mind rather than a consequence of his possessing some Negro genes, nor could he have shown more persuasively that for Joe the notion that he is a Negro is part of his general alienation from the community" (p. vii). In short, Faulkner suggests that Joe becomes a "nigger" because he is treated like one. When Joe asks Joanna Burden why her father did not kill Colonel Sartoris after the Colonel killed her father and his son, Joanna postulates the notion that because her father was half French, he understood "that a man [like Sartoris] would have to act as the land where he was born had trained him to act" (p. 241). When the Reverend Gail Hightower tells Byron Bunch that he did not choose to leave the ministry, he says: "It was by the will, the more than behest, of them like you and like her [Lena Grove] and like him [Joe Christmas] in the jail yonder and like them who put him there to do their will upon, as they did upon me, with insult and violence. . . . It was not my choice." Byron answers, "I know that. Because a man aint given that many choices. . . . And I reckon them that are good must suffer for it the same as them that are bad" (p. 345).

If Faulkner gives man little choice when confronted by the forces of society or his training, Wright gives Bigger Thomas almost none.

Boris Max, the Party lawyer who defends Bigger, articulates Wright's view. He tells the prosecuting attorney that he is defending Bigger because he is "convinced that men like [the attorney] made him what he is" (p. 271). Certainly Bigger "could never tell why he had killed. It was not that he did not really want to tell, but that [as in the case of Joe Christmas] the telling of it would have involved an explanation of his entire life" (p. 286). At the trial, Max offers an explanation of Bigger's conduct based on the Marxist idea that social evil results from the conscious or unconscious exploitation of the masses to create luxury for the few (p. 357). The blacks at the bottom of society "were engaged in a struggle for life and their choice in the matter was small indeed" (p. 359). Therefore, Bigger's "entire attitude toward life is a *crime!* The hate and fear which we have inspired in him, woven by our civilization into the very structure of his consciousness, into his blood and bones, into the hourly functioning of his personality, have become the justification of his existence" (pp. 366–67).

But, interestingly enough, both Faulkner and Wright allow for some free will and therefore some hope. And in both cases an ability to choose depends upon one's knowledge of self. When Joanna Burden asks Joe Christmas how he knows he is "part nigger," he says "I don't know it." Then he adds, "If I'm not, damned if I haven't wasted a lot of time" (pp. 240–41). That is, by implication he is not absolutely forced to be what he is; on some level he has chosen to act as he does. Surely Gail Hightower elects to return to life when he delivers Lena Grove's baby. Similarly, once Bigger Thomas understands that he does not have to take upon himself "the crime of being black" (p. 275) because he is not responsible for that "crime," he can accept some responsibility for his individual acts, break down some of the barriers of isolation, and confess to Max that he "never wanted to hurt nobody," that he "didn't want to kill" (pp. 388, 391). The implication at the end of *Native Son* is that despite social forces which have made him into "just a scared colored boy from Mississippi," Bigger's new knowledge of himself and society would have allowed him to live differently. Nor is self-knowledge a social force. It is, rather, the one aspect of our common humanity that allows us "to repent, believe, and be baptized" if we are Christians, which allows us to make deliberate, conscious, moral choices no matter who we are. It is the presence of this limited self-knowledge that affords Bigger the sense of identity as a human being he has been seeking throughout the novel. It is finally the absence of any real sense of his actual identity that forces Joe Christmas, when fleeing the posse, to put on the Negro brogans and symbolically accept identity as a black man.

Despite its Marxist attitudes and literary naturalism, Wright's novel is clearly the work of a southern as well as a native son. His use of material from his younger years in Jackson; of the Gothic, the grotesque, the violent; of the protagonist as inverted Christ figure; his concern with questions of free will and determinism; his study of black-white relationships: all are the common concerns of Faulkner and the other major southern novelists. As in the case of Chesnutt, Johnson, and Toomer, it is not that Wright is deliberately echoing Faulkner, or that McCullers, Capote, and O'Connor are deliberately borrowing from Wright. Rather, all of them are part of a southern literary tradition. That Wright's intent was to write in the mode of Dreiser and the other American Naturalists while his finest novel has so many of the characteristics identified with works in the southern literary canon argues for the fundamental unity of those elements of southern culture—black and white—out of which these novelists write.

That *Black Boy* so closely—and I would say so deliberately— echoes, cites, paraphrases, and follows the example of *Look Homeward, Angel* suggests that Wright was conscious not only that he was a southerner, but that he too was a southern novelist; that as a southern writer as well as a product of the South, Wright represented "that rare thing we sometimes call a clear case."

VI

The Shadow of the Past
Ralph Ellison, 1914–

The act of writing requires a constant plunging
back into the shadow of the past where time hovers
ghost-like.

> —Ralph Ellison, *Shadow and Act*

Born in Oklahoma City in 1914, the son of a Georgia mother and a father who died when he was three, Ralph Ellison is one of the major writers, of whatever origin, to appear since 1945. A talented trumpeter, in his youth Ellison developed an interest in both jazz and Western classical music.[1] After studying music for three years at the Tuskegee Institute (whose faculty included the distinguished composer William Dawson), the young Ellison came to New York in 1936, where he worked with the Federal Writers Project and became a friend of Richard Wright. As his interest in literature grew, he increasingly devoted himself to writing. A staff member of the *Negro Quarterly* in the early 1940s, Ellison was also publishing pieces in *New Masses* and *The New Republic*. In 1952 he published *Invisible Man*, a novel that at least one critic ranks "with *Absalom, Absalom!* and *The Sound and the Fury* among the great novels of twentieth-century America."[2] Undoubtedly it is one of the most honored and widely read. It is the only work by a Negro to have won a National Book award. In 1965 some two hundred authors, critics, and editors responding to a *Book Week* poll judged it the most distinguished single work published in the previous twenty years, a period which also saw the appearance of *All the King's Men, Lie Down in Darkness, The Naked and the Dead, A Member of the Wedding, Go Tell It on the Mountain, The Assistant, The Adventures of Augie March, Herzog, The Catcher in the Rye,* and *Rabbit, Run.* In 1964 Ellison published *Shadow and Act,* a collection of reviews and essays that contains the raw materials for his intellectual autobiography. Widely honored as a writer and lecturer (he has received the Medal of Freedom, several honorary degrees, and is a Chevalier de l'Ordre des Arts et Lettres), Ellison continues to write as he serves as the Albert Schweitzer Professor of Humanities at New York University. He has not, unhappily, produced a second novel.

Oklahoma a southern state? Ralph Ellison a southern writer? Oklahoma was not even a state in 1860, much less a member of the Confederacy. During the time of the Civil War the only southern literary figure who might have been there was Huck Finn; otherwise it was the Indian Territory inhabited primarily by the Cherokees, Creeks, Seminoles, Choctaws, and Chickasaws who moved there from the southeastern states. And although the Indians brought slaves with them, furnished a brigade that fought for the South (the Cherokee Stand Watie became a Confederate brigadier general), and lost their land as a result of their alliance with the Confederacy, such a past hardly casts the kind of shadow that would mark Oklahoma as a southern state. Much more important was the settling there after the war of many newly freed men and former Confederates. During Ellison's early years, the Alabama-born Robert L. Williams was governor of the state. An ardent white supremacist, Williams sponsored the "grandfather clause" that became an amendment to the Oklahoma constitution. During the 1920s the Ku Klux Klan was such a powerful political force that it controlled many elections, especially at the local level. Thus the Oklahoma of the 1930s (the period governed by "Alfalfa Bill" Murray), while hardly comparable in its social arrangements to Mississippi, Alabama, and the other Deep South states, was as Ellison knew it a segregated society. And while it was not the agrarian South of his mother's Georgia, it was still agrarian enough for Ellison to remember seeing black children leave school during the cotton-picking season to work with their parents in the fields.[3]

It seems to me that during Ellison's formative years, Oklahoma was a southern state to almost the same degree that Missouri was when Samuel Clemens was growing up. Belonging neither to the Tidewater nor the Deep South, the inhabitants of both areas resemble those described by C. Hugh Holman in his discussion of the Piedmont and Mountain South: "Their pragmatic view of life, their folk-version Calvinism, and their anti-intellectual individualism created a special world favorable to egalitarian democracy and having little patience with and no respect for aristocratic pretensions. This cotton country and hill country, made up of small farms, small towns, and small cities spaced very far apart, maintains to this day many of its early characteristics."[4] Holman describes the Piedmont society as being "in many ways more nearly American and less distinctively Southern" than other southern regions. More recently, Louis D. Rubin, Jr., has extended his friend Holman's description of the Piedmont to include the region of Twain's Missouri. "The farmlands of eastern Missouri are not part of the Piedmont, but in the days when Samuel L. Clemens was growing up there, they were surely the border south."[5] And the presence of so many settlers, black and white, from the deep South, the strength of the KKK, the voting in of grandfather clauses, and the practice of racial segregation argue that like those of Samuel Clemens's Hannibal, Missouri, the interests, tastes, and attitudes of Ralph Ellison's Oklahoma City were notably southern.

Professor Rubin includes Ralph Ellison along with Mark Twain in his *Bibliographical Guide to the Study of Southern Literature* (1969). Ellison shared a platform in 1968 with William Styron and Robert Penn Warren at the Southern Historical Association meeting in New Orleans as a member of a panel moderated by C. Vann Woodward, which suggests that Rubin is not alone in this judgment. Most importantly, Ellison considers himself a southerner:

That's one of the advantages of a Southern upbringing: a lot of things which got lost up here were not lost back there. I mean just

things you took for granted, things I assumed everybody knew. . . .
Well, *I'm* from the South. . . .

. . . I believe that a black Southern writer who does know his traditions has some of the advantages which William Faulkner or other
white Southern writers have had: the advantage of contact with a
long accumulation of history in a given place; an experience which
has been projected in other forms of artistic expression, which has
traditional values and variants, and which has been refined by being
defined by generations of people who have told what it seemed to
be: *"This is the life of black men here. . . ."*
What we have in the South is an oral tradition which extends
right back into slavery and which has been projected in terms of
archetypal characters: John the Slave, John Henry, Stagolee—a
whole group of them—and they're real-life versions of local characters. People know them by word of mouth rather than their having
been written about. . . .
This is one of the advantages of the South. In the stories you get
the texture of an experience and the projection of values, and the
distillation of a kind of wisdom.[6]

Certainly Ellison's self-description could be applied with few
modifications to almost any major modern writer from the South.
And in describing himself, Ellison isolates the southern elements
within *Invisible Man* that I want to explore with some care: the
sense of the past and its importance in defining an individual's identity; the use of an oral tradition and folk materials; and the projection of values that distill into a kind of wisdom.

In his most recent book (one that will surely join *The Roots of
Southern Writing* and *Three Modes of Southern Fiction* as required
reading for any serious student of southern literature), C. Hugh
Holman examines the relationship between history, the past, and
the southern writer.

The imagination of the southerner for over one hundred and sev-
enty-five years has been historical. The imagination of the Puritans
was essentially typological, catching fire as it saw men and events as
types of Christian principles. The imagination of the New England
romantics was fundamentally symbolic, translating material objects
into ideal forms and ideas. The southerner has always had his imaginative faculties excited by events in time and has found the most
profound truths of the present and the future in the interpretation
of the past.[7]

Arguing that the dominant American way of seeing history is to view it in "Nietzschean terms of endless replication through each individual of the universal racial experience," a view of history that denies any overarching values, Holman defines the southern view of the past as essentially Hegelian, an attitude that sees history in "terms of pattern, of change, in which ultimate meanings are functions of the process and not of the individual events."[8]

As he explores the implication of this Hegelian notion that history, the past, almost inevitably means something to the southerner, Holman divides southern writers into three camps. There are those like William Gilmore Simms, who in the vein of Sir Walter Scott wrote historical novels to show what the past means and how its lessons should be applied. As my earlier discussion suggests, Charles Chesnutt's novels belong in this camp. There are those like Ellen Glasgow, who in the vein of Henry James wrote realistic social history (in Glasgow's case, a history tracing the change of Virginia from an aristocratic to a commercial society). To a limited degree, James Weldon Johnson and Richard Wright wrote in this vein. More obviously, Ernest Gaines's *Jane Pittman*, William Attaway's *Blood on the Forge*, and Margaret Walker's *Jubilee* belong with the works constituting this group. And there are those like Faulkner and Robert Penn Warren, who have used the modern novelistic form with its disjunctures of time, experimental styles and structures, nondiscursive narrative methods, improbable actions, etc., "to describe a world of essentially allegorical meanings."[9] Ellison's *Invisible Man* belongs among the very best works of this last group. It also shares the southern writer's characteristic concern with and attitude toward the past.

In the prologue to *Invisible Man*, Ellison establishes the symbolism implicit in his title.[10] His nameless narrator is invisible because when people look at him they do not see him as an individual. Rather, they see his surroundings, the color of his skin, projections of themselves, figures of their imaginations, a representative of a class—anything and everything but the narrator as person. As the novel begins, the narrator has withdrawn to a forgotten underground New York basement surrealistically illuminated by exactly 1,369 lightbulbs on power stolen from Monopolated Light. Although the novel itself explains the events that have caused him to move underground, the prologue suggests Ellison's intentions as well as some of his debts to his literary relatives and ancestors. The conceit of a narrator who is invisible is a logical extension of Johnson's conceit of a narrator who "passes" in the *Autobiography of an Ex-Coloured Man*. The metaphor of a black man's subterranean withdrawal is a brilliant modification of Wright's more nearly realistic treatment in "The Man Who Lived Underground." In both instances, Ellison has "done his robberies so openly, that . . . what would be theft in other poets, is only victory in him." For Ellison, the "hole in the ground" is a place where, like Jack the Bear (who, in Duke Ellington's song, "ain't nowhere") and Jack Burden, his narrator hibernates. Not a grave, it is a warm womblike place from which he will ultimately emerge "like the Easter chick breaking from its shell" (p. 5). It is a place where in a state of suspended animation his memory can know before knowing can remember and contemplate those elements of his racial and personal past that will allow him to be himself, to define his own identity. As he listens to Louis Armstrong singing Fats Waller's "What Did I Do to Be So Black and Blue?" (and with allusions to the hell of Dante, the unheard music of Keats, and the Freudian primal crime), the narrator recalls images of the past: a naked slave girl at auction with a voice like his mother's; a Negro sermon on the "Blackness of Blackness"; the voice of an old spiritual singer, who, like Job's wife, first tells him to curse God and die and then affirms her own simultaneous love of the white master who gave her several sons and her hatred of him for keeping her enslaved; the memory of Ras the Destroyer and Brother Jack, figures from his own experience. These images recall instances from his past as a descendant of black slaves and white masters, his cultural present as expressed through the blues, and his recent experiences with Ras and Brother Jack. It is out of the interconnections among these levels of his past that the invisible man can find self-visibility and, therefore, self-identity in the present and future.

Jack Burden, Warren's narrator in *All the King's Men* (1946), demonstrates his understanding that all time is one time, that one cannot have the future unless one understands and accepts the past—

in part through his memory, which juxtaposes experiences not only from different periods in his own life but also from the plantation and Civil War life of his supposed relative Cass Mastern.[11]

The invisible man demonstrates that he has learned a similar lesson through his memory of his grandfather's life and death, a memory that comes to his consciousness at key times throughout the novel as a commentary on the narrator's present. After living an exemplary life of apparent humility in accordance with the white southern view of what a "good nigger" should be, the grandfather says on his deathbed that he has been fighting all of his life as a spy in the enemy's country. He says that the "Young 'uns" must learn "to overcome 'em with yeses, undermine 'em with grins, agree 'em to death and destruction, let 'em swoller you till they vomit or bust wide open" (pp. 13–14). Ashamed of his grandfather for having been a slave and unable as yet to understand his meaning, the invisible man rejects his teaching and lives instead by a southern black myth as false in its way as the southern white myth of a golden time in which benign masters sipped mint juleps while happy darkies strummed banjos and noble sons and virtuous daughters lived lives of gallant idealism. The black myth is the myth of the Negro as one whose station is now inferior but who will eventually rise to attain professional and social success once he has proved himself worthy through patience, education, and hard work. It is the myth preached by Booker T. Washington and to some degree accepted and lived by Charles W. Chesnutt and James Weldon Johnson. And just as Faulkner's *Absalom, Absalom!*, *Light in August*, and "A Rose for Emily," Warren's *All the King's Men*, Styron's *Lie Down in Darkness*, and Flannery O'Connor's "A Late Encounter with the Enemy" are all works that in one way or another attack the present validity of the white southern myth, Ellison's *Invisible Man* annihilates the black one.

Before he can discover that he is "nobody but himself," the invisible man thinks he is a black Horatio Alger. His speech as class valedictorian quotes directly from Booker T. Washington's "cast down your bucket" address given at the 1895 Atlanta Exposition, an address in which Washington urged the Negro to accept work "in agriculture, mechanics, in commerce, in domestic service, and in the professions. . . . to keep in mind that we shall prosper in propor-

tion as we learn to dignify and glorify common labour and put
brains and skill into the common occupations of life. . . . It is at the
bottom of life we must begin, and not at the top." Washington also
promised whites that "in all things that are purely social we can be
separate as the fingers, yet one as the hand in all things essential to
mutual progress."[12] Washington's speech was an important event in
the invisible man's past. The advice he offered may well have been
necessary for the Negro to survive during the early twentieth century. But it became the basis of a treacherous myth.

In the chapter that presents the invisible man's life in the South,
Ellison attacks this myth in a variety of ways. He attacks it by having his protagonist deliver his own version of Washington's speech
to the town's white leadership in a hotel ballroom. But rather than
finding dignity through respect for his attainments, the invisible
man is humiliated by seeing the white man's sexual fantasies projected on him and on the other young black men present, first by
being forced to fight his fellow blacks while blindfolded, and finally
by scrabbling after false coins placed on an electrified blanket symbolic of American society, symbolic of the false promises and jolting
shocks which the Negro will eventually discover is its nature. The
result is a humiliating loss of dignity at the very time he is trying to
play the game by the rules of the myth. For his pains he is given a
calfskin briefcase in which he is to keep the important objects that
will help shape the destiny of his people.

The Booker T. Washington myth is attacked when the protagonist
goes off to a college patently modeled on Washington's (and Ellison's) Tuskegee. There is even a description of the Booker T. Washington memorial located at Tuskegee, with the Founder's hands
"outstretched in the breathtaking gesture of lifting a veil . . . above
the face of a kneeling slave." The narrator wonders "whether the
veil is really being lifted, or lowered more firmly in place" (p. 28).
Although the campus appears to be a green garden of Eden in
which blacks can learn to improve themselves, to the narrator it
becomes a flower-studded wasteland—a broken and corroded foun-
tain, which, echoing T. S. Eliot, is visited by "oh, oh, oh, those
multimillionaires," and whose apparent king, Bledsoe, retains his
potency only by paying obeisance to the white power represented
by Norton, the college trustee. Ellison's use of the wasteland meta-

phor to comment on the discrepancy between the entrance into life promised by the college and the actual sterility it gives parallels its use by Faulkner, Styron, and other twentieth-century southern novelists. Ellison uses the image to comment on the inadequacy of the black southern myth. Faulkner uses it in *Sartoris/Flags in the Dust* to comment on the inadequacy of the white southern myth as represented by Colonel John's and his brother's gallant Civil War exploits, a myth by which young Bayard cannot live in the South to which he returns after World War I. In *Sanctuary* Faulkner uses the wasteland within which the loathly Miss Reba's whorehouse stands as an emblem of what Temple Drake has become, the ironic contemporary avatar of "that most sacred thing in life: womanhood." In *Lie Down in Darkness* (1951), Styron uses the wasteland through which Milton Loftis rides with his dead daughter Peyton, representative of all meaning, to show Milton's empty life and values. For each of these southern writers, the wasteland represents in part the false dead myth by which the twentieth-century southerner, black or white, has tried to live; from which he has gained his identity; within which, ultimately, lie the seeds of his destruction.

Like Jack Burden, the narrator of *Invisible Man* cannot see the full meaning of events until later when he can look back upon their direction; he must, therefore, live through a series of experiences before he can reject the false black myth. His disillusionment begins when he takes Mr. Norton, whose incestuous feelings for his dead daughter are no better concealed than those of Milton Loftis, to the home of Trueblood, an ignorant black sharecropper who represents many of the aspects of black life which the college authorities wish to hide and forget. In bed with his wife and daughter to escape the cold weather, a half-asleep Trueblood has impregnated his daughter, thereby becoming a scapegoat for the unadmitted impulses of the whites, or rather, one to whom Norton and the others can pay guilt money. Trueblood's response to this almost Oedipal situation, in which abominable incest is committed without deliberate intent, is to fall back upon the black man's true past. Instinctively, he says, "I *ends up* singin' the blues . . . and, while I'm singin' them blues I makes up my mind that I ain't nobody but myself and ain't nothing I can do but let whatever is gonna happen, happen" (p. 51). Thus, unlike the narrator until late in the novel,

Trueblood accepts his past, his identity both as a black man and as
an individual human being.

If in the present Trueblood can confront chaos and retain his san-
ity through recourse to an experience from his cultural heritage,
those blacks who have attempted to live by the black Horatio Alger
myth find madness instead. To revive Mr. Norton, who has col-
lapsed after the Trueblood experience, the narrator takes him to the
Golden Day, a bar frequented by the inhabitants of a nearby sanitarium for shell-shocked war veterans. Made up of black men who
have been doctors, lawyers, teachers, civil service workers, cooks,
preachers, politicians, and artists, the patients "were supposed to
be members of the professions toward which at various times I
vaguely aspired myself" (p. 57). But instead of the respect, recognition, and dignity that they hoped to attain through education and
work, these men had been abused, rebuked, and scorned wherever
they had tried to practice their professions. Appropriately, they
have entered a sanitarium either because they have gone mad, or
(and this is Ellison's point) the established social order is itself
insane.

Inside the Golden Day, chaos reigns. Intoxicated with alcohol
and sex, the vets overthrow Supercargo, their attendant. Mr. Norton is identified by one of the inmates as his grandfather Thomas
Jefferson, an ironic allusion to the miscegenation allegedly prac-
ticed by Mr. Jefferson, an aspect of the heroic southern myth usually ignored by whites (other than Robert Penn Warren). One of the
vets attends Mr. Norton, his medical skill self-evident. When asked
why he had given up medicine, the profession he had worked so
hard to enter, the vet explains that he sought dignity and a chance
to help his fellow man, but was allowed neither. He demonstrates
that those who live by the black myth either develop ulcers and
frustration, go mad in despair, or become like the narrator at this
time: an invisible automaton, one who believes that "white is right,"
who sees himself as "a thing and not a man" (pp. 72–73).

Expelled from college for exposing Norton to Trueblood and the
Golden Day, the narrator sees that he is losing the only identity he
has ever known, not because he sees that the college is a wasteland,
but because he still accepts the southern black myth and wants to
become a great Negro leader like Bledsoe, the school president.

Even though the narrator realizes that Bledsoe is a lying hypocrite, a petty tyrant, a completely selfish man who is treating him unfairly, he cannot reject Bledsoe as a model. After all, he is influential, a leader of people, makes a good salary, has power and authority, and owns two Cadillacs (p. 78).

Before the narrator leaves, he attends a chapel program at which "the black rite of Horatio Alger was performed to God's own acting script." The program is clearly an act of religious communion among all those united in the faith, performed not with "the wafer and the wine," but with "the flesh and the blood" of millionaires come down to portray themselves (p. 87). In a sermon as blasphemous in its way as the Reverend Gail Hightower's in *Light in August*, which celebrates the false myth of his grandfather's heroic death, the Reverend Homer A. Barbee preaches of the Christlike life of the Founder and his struggle upward from slavery to celebrate the black myth embodied in the life and teachings of Booker T. Washington. Using the evocative rhetorical techniques of the black evangelist, Barbee moves his listeners to respond to and accept the false gospel of HOPE, FAITH, ENDURANCE, and TRIUMPH based on a belief in the Founder and trust in Bledsoe, his successor. It is a bravura performance, marred only by the revelation that Barbee is sightless, a physically blind man leading the spiritually blind. Ellison's attitude toward the myth is suggested afterward when the narrator sees a mockingbird flipping its tail over the head of the eternally kneeling slave on the Founder's monument. The act is a telling commentary on this meretricious southern myth; the revelation that Hightower's grandfather was killed robbing a chicken house is a similar commentary on the other, equally meretricious, myth. The fact that he feels "his grandfather . . . hovering over [him], grinning triumphantly out of the dark" (p. 113) as he prepares to leave the college is both a reminder of the narrator's true past—the past he must accept before he can discover himself—and an indication that the narrator is learning, willingly or not, one aspect of the false myth.

Despite the example of his grinning grandfather and the precept of the vet, who warns him to leave the Mr. Nortons alone and to become his own father—that is, to discover and define himself (p. 120)—the invisible man continues to live by the Horatio Alger/

Booker T. Washington myth—even to the extent of being concerned about parting his hair on the right side and using the proper deodorant. He still wants to be a younger, more charming Bledsoe with a voice like Ronald Colman's. More importantly, he carries with him some of the emblems of his personal past inside the briefcase he won for delivering his valedictory address. That he also carries these emblems as memories inside himself is shown when he picks up a Gideon Bible, thinks of his father's church-house rhetoric, and is homesick (pp. 120, 124–25).

Carrying letters of introduction from Bledsoe which are in truth letters of betrayal, he begins the second stage of his adventure in Algerism: he looks for work. He has learned Booker T. Washington's lesson that common labor is worthy of dignity and glory. He has been advised by Mr. Norton to read Emerson, that apostle of self-reliant individualism, infinite possibility, and American scholarship whose transcendentalism came partly from Carlyle, himself an evangelist of "the perennial nobleness, and even sacredness of work." Work is noble and sacred, however, only if one has a job, and Bledsoe's letters insure that none is available to the protagonist. On his way with his last letter to an interview with a "Mr. Emerson," who seems to be able to provide his final opportunity to realize the false myth, the narrator passes a blues-singing, jive-talking man pushing a cart. The man reawakens elements of the past that have given black men the strength to endure. When the narrator momentarily fails to understand some of the jive talk, the blues singer says: "Now I know you from down home, how come you trying to act like you never heard that before! Hell, ain't nobody out here this morning but us colored. Why you trying to deny me?" (p. 132). And the narrator begins to respond to the cart man's "shit, grit and mother-wit," with a combination of amusement, pride, and disgust. Even so, like Jack Burden who cannot accept what is to him an ugly past represented by a weak father and a loveless mother, the invisible man cannot accept a past represented by his grandfather, Trueblood, or the cart man. Instead, when he enters a drugstore and is offered a southern breakfast of pork chops, grits, egg, biscuits, and coffee, he coldly asks for a blandly inferior Yankee breakfast of orange juice, toast, and coffee, food from which he gets no pleasure and little nourishment (p. 135).

Only after Mr. Emerson's son (a weak, father-dominated northern liberal who says "Some of the finest people I know are Neg——") allows him to read Bledsoe's letter is the narrator disillusioned. He sees that the Booker T. Washington myth is false and that he has no identity within it. His response is the same as Trueblood's and the cart man's. He instinctively sings the blues he remembers from his youth.

> O well they picked poor Robin clean
> O well they picked poor Robin clean
> Well they tied poor Robin to a stump
>   Lawd, they picked all the feathers round from Robin's rump
> Well they picked poor Robin clean. (p. 147)

On a conscious level, he has begun to turn to those roots in the past that will help him define himself as a person. He does not yet see, however, that all definitions from outside himself are suspect. As he passes through a series of episodes, the narrator continues to seek an identity that conforms to a view imposed by others. Like Jack Burden, the narrator learns a little more each time about the inadequacy of the view he has adopted. Also like Jack Burden, the narrator is forced at the end toward a definition of himself based on an understanding and acceptance of the past.

Through Emerson the younger, the narrator gets a job at a paint factory. No longer ambitious to be a notable black man like Bledsoe, he just wants to do his job and mind his own business. Instead of being offered transcendental dignity, however, he is identified both as a scab by the union members and as a troublemaker by those opposed to the union. Factory work, the industrial experience, northern attitudes and expectations, all are assaults on the invisible man's sense of identity. Like the Booker T. Washington myth of upward mobility, the Washington myth of noble manual labor is also shown to be specious. After a factory explosion, the narrator is reduced to a state where he can function neither physically nor mentally by electric shock treatments at the company hospital that are intended both to castrate and lobotomize him. His identity is so shattered that he cannot even remember his name. But he is saved by his recollection of Buckeye the Rabbit, black folk songs, the dozens, the blues—again all elements of his southern Negro past. Able at last to acknowledge that the black myth is false and irrelevant, he can ask himself who he is, and how he has come to be. That is, he can turn from defining himself according to some preconception to defining himself through self-discovery.

He begins answering the question when he meets a man selling "hot, baked Car'lina yams" on the street, and with the smell inhales memories of cooking them at home and eating them at school. Eating the yam on the street, he no longer feels obligated to deny what he truly enjoys or to live by a code of counterfeit gentility: "To hell with being ashamed of what you liked. No more of that for me. I am what I am! . . . They're my birthmark . . . I yam what I am!" (pp. 200–201). He answers the question further when he looks at and accepts as meaningful to himself the free papers, minstrel show "knocking bones," small Ethiopian flag, picture of Abe Lincoln, and portrait of Marcus Garvey among the street-piled possessions of an old black couple being evicted from their apartment. He is looking at the emblems and artifacts of Negro life as it actually has been lived since emancipation, not the false emblems of Norton and Bledsoe.

Powerfully moved, he delivers a sidewalk speech that inspires the gathered crowd to stop the eviction. Spotted as an effective speaker by Brother Jack, the leader of a local chapter of a Marxist organization called the Brotherhood, the narrator is invited to work as a spokesman and organizer in Harlem. Accepting the job because he needs the money rather than out of any commitment to Marxism, the invisible man is given a new identity and a new myth of history by which to live. He has already accepted too much of the truth of his own past, however, to accept fully a concept of brotherhood that denies the value of either the individual or his particular cultural experience. To the Brotherhood he is, furthermore, neither Negro nor American; he is simply a resource. He knows that he tried to help the black couple because he identified with them as a southern black man, not because of some dialectical concept of history or awareness of economic class. His grandfather is too powerful a presence in his life to allow him to accept a view that denies the value of the dead or of those whom history has passed by, a view that insists on a coldly objective, materialistic understanding of history and its forces (pp. 232–54). Although he cannot as yet acknowledge it, he half knows with Faulkner's Gavin Stevens that "the past is not dead. It's never even past." His experience has already taught him the interconnectedness between time past and time present, between men living then and now, that *Absalom, Absalom!* is based upon and that the background information given in the appendix of *The Sound and the Fury* demonstrates. In short, his attitude toward the past and its meaning is too consciously southern to allow him ever to accept the Marxist myth as completely as he had that of the black South.

Thus, although he accepts the new identity given him by the Brotherhood and cuts himself off physically from the past by changing his place of residence, psychologically he cannot escape the dissenting, disbelieving presence of his grandfather (p. 254). And when he attends his first political rally, he responds to the experience as a southerner rather than as a Marxist. The mood is that of a southern revival meeting (p. 257), and he consciously falls back upon black southern rhetorical devices and the tradition he had heard "so often at home: The old down-to-earth, I'm-sick-and-tired-of-the-way-they've-been-treating-us approach" (p. 259). It is a speech much like Willie Stark's in *All the King's Men*, stressing the extent to which speaker and audience share a common exploitation. Its rhetorical patterns are those of repetition, evocation, biblical allusions, and folk images; and the communal interaction that it creates between speaker and audience is that of a southern Protestant evangelistic meeting. At the end of the speech the narrator feels "more human," because even though ostensibly speaking for the Brotherhood, he has actually affirmed his own cultural and individual past. As he sees this, he remembers also an attitude that he heard expressed in a college lecture on Joyce, an attitude that will prevent him from ever fully belonging to the Brotherhood: "Stephen's problem, like ours, was not actually one of creating the uncreated conscience of his race, but of creating the *uncreated features of his face.* Our task is that of making ourselves individuals. The conscience of a race is the gift of its individuals who see, evaluate, record. . . . We create the race by creating ourselves and then to our great astonishment we will have created something far more important: We will have created a culture" (p. 268). Although the teacher's lecture does not fully explain what the narrator means by "more human," it clearly states an attitude that permeates Ellison's novel. It also suggests the level of self-consciousness that the narrator has now reached, a level that allows him to explain the implications of his own statements and thoughts as well as those of others. "Did I mean that I had become less of what I was, less a Negro, or that I was less a being apart; less an exile from down home, the South?" And in a passage recalling Jack Burden's metaphysical paradoxes, he adds, "But all this is negative. To become less—in order to become more? Perhaps that was it, but in what way *more* human? . . . It was a mystery once more, as at the eviction I had uttered words that had possessed me. . . . For the first time, lying there in the dark, I could glimpse the possibility of being more than a member of a race" (pp. 267–68).

While working for the Brotherhood, the invisible man also rejects the myth of black nationalism represented by a Marcus Garvey–like figure named Ras the Destroyer. Ras affirms an African tribal past as the basis for the black man's identity and attacks the Negro members of the Brotherhood as traitors working for the white enslaver. Unlike the hypocritical Bledsoe, Norton, and Brother Jack, Ras is unquestionably sincere. But even though the African past is truly a part of the black American's heritage to which he responds profoundly (witness Alex Haley's *Roots*), it is not a past by which he can live in twentieth-century America. Ellison has been saying such in his own voice for many years. "'He came to Oberlin in April of 1969,' a black girl in Seattle recalled. 'His speech was about how black culture had blended into American white culture. . . . I think he's very gutsy, in a day like today with all these so-called militants trying to run him into the ground, coming to Oberlin saying to the kids: "You are American, not African."'"[13] He says it in *Invisible Man* by having Ras appear on a big black horse with a fur cap and lion skin over his shoulders in the middle of a Harlem riot commanding the blacks there to rise up and destroy the whites. His sincerity, bravery, but utter irrelevance are shown as he rides "bookety-bookety with that spear stuck out in front of him and that shield on his arm," charging the New York police (p. 425). The other blacks consider him crazy. His attempt to defeat a modern police force with weapons from a tribal past can only fail. Ras's myth of an African identity for twentieth-century American blacks is ultimately as pernicious to Ellison as the myth of Ivanhoe for nineteenth-century southern whites was to Mark Twain. If accepted and followed to its conclusion, the former will lead at best to isolation from what is meaningful to blacks in our national life, at worst to destruction; when accepted and followed to its logical conclusion, the latter led, in Twain's view, to the War Between the States.

The invisible man finds one person within the Brotherhood who ties him to his true roots. This is Brother Tarp, an escaped convict who identifies for him a picture of Frederick Douglass, the escaped slave who defined himself, named himself, and became a great man. Douglass, not the Founder, Bledsoe, or Ras, points the way to a valid black American identity. Moreover, his accomplishments are fact, not myth. Brother Tarp, in whose eyes the narrator sees his grandfather, tells the story of his own imprisonment and escape and gives the narrator a piece of the chain that had been shackled to his leg. The invisible man puts it in his briefcase. The narrator sees this gesture as "something, perhaps, like a man passing on to his son his own father's watch, which the son accepted not because he wanted the old-fashioned time-piece for itself, but because of the overtones of unstated seriousness and solemnity of the paternal gesture which at once joined him with his ancestors, marked a high point of his present, and promised a concreteness to his nebulous and chaotic future" (p. 294). Quentin Compson went through the same rite of passage when his father gave him General Compson's watch. For Quentin the gesture is without value because to him the watch is merely a mechanical measure of man's meaningless existence. In *Go Down, Moses* Sam Fathers's baptizing Ike McCaslin with the blood of the first deer Ike has been worthy enough to kill suggests the same juncture of present with past embodied in Tarp's gift. Ellison and Faulkner obviously share a common vision of the importance of relatives and ancestors in defining ourselves and discovering meaning in the present.

After a policeman murders his friend Tod Clifton, the invisible man questions the official party doctrine regarding both history and the individual. "What if history was a gambler, instead of a force in a laboratory experiment?" (p. 333). Like Jack Burden, who concludes that although history is morally blind, man has free will because he is not, the narrator decides that even if politically the individual is meaningless, he is valuable as a human being (p. 337). This is the basis of the sermon he preaches as an act of personal responsibility at Tod Clifton's funeral to a crowd he sees as composed of individual men and women (p. 347). The narrator's views are now so obviously in opposition to those of the Brotherhood that he decides to follow his grandfather's advice and "yes 'em to death" as a spy in the enemy camp. Instead, during the Harlem riot fomented by the unscrupulous Brotherhood he is driven underground to hibernate alone with his briefcase.

In his five-page epilogue, however, the narrator goes back to his grandfather's instruction to "yes 'em to death" and decides that his ancestor must have meant for him to affirm and take responsibility for the principle upon which the country was built and reject the men who have betrayed the principle. Although Ellison never explicitly states this principle, he clearly means the self-evident truth that all men are created equal. Like Jack Burden, who at the end of *All the King's Men* finds his personal identity partly because he can affirm a web theory of human interrelationships, the narrator can find his personal identity partly because he can affirm that "we, through no fault of our own, [are] linked to all the others in the loud, clamoring semi-visible world" (p. 434). Like Faulkner's Judith Sutpen, who knows that life "can't matter . . . and yet it must matter because you keep on trying," the narrator also echoes the French existentialists in asserting that "life is to be lived, not controlled; and humanity is won by continuing to play in face of certain defeat" (p. 435). He defends his decision to participate in the pain and evil of our national life because, like Quentin Compson and the South, the narrator both loves and hates it (pp. 437–38). But unlike Quentin, whose final act in *Absalom, Absalom!* is to deny that he hates the South and whose inability to find a meaning from the past by which he can live leads to his suicide in *The Sound and the Fury*, the invisible man's final act is to affirm that which is valuable in American life and denounce that which is not. And out of this intermingling of love and hate, he affirms his own identity as an individual who is black, American, and above all human. Like Jack Burden awakening from one of his great sleeps, the narrator will soon leave his hibernation to return to the "convulsion of the world, out of his-

tory into history and the awful responsibility of *Time*." When he
leaves he will take with him his briefcase full of artifacts, among
them the chain link given him by Tarp; that is, he will take symbolic
reminders of his actual history and his true past rather than meaningless tokens from the past of some false myth.

Ellison uses history in ways analogous to all three of those defined by Professor Holman. Although he does not write a historical
novel in the Simms/Scott vein, he uses the career of his protagonist
to suggest the history of the southern black who has moved from
slavery to Booker T. Washingtonism, to the migrations north, to
Marxism, to (it is hoped) a viable position as a free human individual. Like a Simms novel, *Invisible Man* suggests that these experiences offer understandable meanings if we will but see them. Like
Glasgow or James, Ellison creates a social history that, while not
always narrowly realistic, certainly captures satirically—and frequently humorously—the social manners he wishes to attack; and
like Faulkner, Warren, Styron, and other southern authors, Ellison
uses contemporary novelistic techniques masterfully to body forth
the symbolic meanings he sees in his protagonist's experiences.
Moreover, he creates a cyclical structure for his novel that in itself is
a comment on the nature of man's experience in time. Ellison's evidence of the past's continued presence is embodied in the shadow it
casts through folk elements—the songs, the extravagant language,
the tall-tale, the evangelical Protestantism—that make up the
shared experience of the southerner, both black and white. In Holman's terms, his message is Hegelian. There is meaning in history;
the past is revealed through process, not replication. His voice is
southern. His *Invisible Man* is worthy indeed to claim a place
among the great southern novels of this or any other century.

VII

Products of the Southern Condition

The Negro writer, like the white writer of the South, is
a product of the Southern condition.
—Arna Bontemps,
"The Negro Renaissance: Jean Toomer and the
Harlem Writers of the 1920's"

In this brief study I have not at-
tempted a full and inclusive survey of the major black southern novelists. Many important, worthy writers have indeed been omitted.
But by examining a few selected works written by important and, I
think, representative southern black novelists, I have tried to suggest that a close literary kinship exists between black and white
writers of the South. This relationship is not one of master to slave,
of superior to inferior. Rather, it is a relationship between acknowledged members of a literary family who draw upon the southern
experience to write novels with characteristically southern themes,
using characteristically southern literary devices, reflecting characteristically southern values and attitudes. It is a relationship
between writers produced by the same region who also share common literary ancestors from the national and indeed European
traditions.

Charles Chesnutt's concern with the interplay between past and
present, with questions of free will and identity, with the relation-

ship between black and white are all characteristics of southern fiction. His depiction of the Wilmington riot "to say to his contemporary readers what the past meant and how it should be applied"[1] suggests his specific place within the William Gilmore Simms family of southern writers.

In *The Autobiography of an Ex-Coloured Man*, James Weldon Johnson celebrates folk materials, uses southern Negro rhetorical devices, explores the question of racial identity through a depiction of the mulatto's plight, all recognizably southern literary attributes. His realistic depiction of America's social manners as seen by a "passing" black man associates him with the same branch of the family as Ellen Glasgow and James Branch Cabell.

Jean Toomer's lyrical voice celebrating the fertility figures and natural beauty he identifies with black southern peasant life establishes his membership within the clan of southern romantic poets who worked in prose. His depiction of spiritually paralyzed life in the city, with its grotesque images and repeated failures to communicate, shows a strong strain of the southern Gothic.

Richard Wright's *Black Boy*, written in the autobiographical mode of *Look Homeward, Angel*, with echoes of the language, attitudes, and ideas of that book, strongly suggests that Wright felt a bond with Wolfe. His *Native Son*, with its Gothic symbolism and inverted Christ figures, its exploration of black-white relationships and questions of free will, and its concern with the life of a scared colored boy from Mississippi gives ample evidence of his membership in a literary family that includes Faulkner, Capote, O'Connor, and McCullers.

And *Invisible Man*, with its treatment of the relationship between time past (both mythic and actual) and an individual's present identity, its structural and stylistic experiments, and its occasional depiction of action that can only be called absurd, establishes Ralph Ellison's membership within the family of major contemporary southern novelists which includes Faulkner, Warren, and Styron.

Houston A. Baker's thesis that the black novel comes from a culture that is fundamentally, qualitatively different from white American culture is suspect, simply because there are such relationships at all. That these relationships are so integrally a part of the novels written by black southerners and extend into all of the major areas of southern literary concern suggests that for these writers the South is much more than what Frederick J. Hoffman terms a sociological, psychological, and moral reference point. And John M. Bradbury's judgment that there has not been a southern black literary renaissance is true only if one segregates the southern black writer and his work from the southern white writer and his. In my judgment, however, the southern black novelist is just as much a part of a twentieth-century southern literary renascence as he is of a twentieth-century black literary renaissance. Remarkably indeed, this renascence has taken place during a time when the black southern writer was not only socially segregated from the southern white writers, but largely denied access to the usual intellectual resources. Perhaps this last is not so remarkable after all. Perhaps it is but further evidence of the continued existence of an inverse ratio between the comparative material poverty and the comparative literary wealth of the American South. As we know, literature is created "out of the materials of the human spirit." It deals with "the old universal truths lacking which any story is ephemeral and doomed—love and honor and pity and pride and compassion and sacrifice." The great glory of black and white southern literature is that it meets the test implied by Faulkner. And as we also know, the human spirit "is not so much a color as the . . . absence of color, and at the same time the concrete of all colors."

Notes

Chapter I: *Relatives and Ancestors*

1. A notable exception to this generalization was *Richard Wright*, by Milton and Patricia Rickels (vol. 11, 1970) in the short-lived Southern Writers Series published by Steck-Vaughn of Austin, Texas. Recent anthologies and bibliographies have also tended to be increasingly more inclusive. The relatively early *The Literature of the South*, ed. Thomas Daniel Young, Floyd C. Watkins, and Richmond Croom Beatty (Glenview, Ill.: Scott, Foresman and Co., 1952; 1968), devotes fewer than twenty pages out of more than one thousand to Richard Wright and Booker T. Washington. More recently, *The Southern Experience in Short Fiction*, ed. Allen F. Stein and Thomas N. Walters (Glenview, Ill.: Scott, Foresman and Co., 1971), contains two pieces each by both Wright and Ellison. The indispensable *A Bibliographical Guide to the Study of Southern Literature*, ed. Louis D. Rubin, Jr. (Baton Rouge: Louisiana State University Press, 1969), includes entries for Charles W. Chesnutt, but omits, among others, Arna Bontemps, George Henderson, Zora Neale Hurston, and William Attaway. Since its founding in 1968, *The Southern Literary Journal* has published a number of pieces by and about black southerners.

2. *Renaissance in the South: A Critical History of the Literature, 1920–1960* (Chapel Hill: University of North Carolina Press, 1963), p. 148.

3. *The Art of Southern Fiction: A Study of Some Modern Novelists* (Car-

103

bondale and Edwardsville: Southern Illinois University Press, 1967),
p. 165.

4.   Louis D. Rubin, Jr., "The South and the Faraway Country," in *Writers of the Modern South: The Faraway Country* (Seattle: University of Washington Press, 1966), p. 20.

5.   *Long Black Song: Essays in Black American Literature and Culture* (Charlottesville: University of Virginia Press, 1972), pp. 6, 10, 13, 15–16.

6.   *The Negro Novel in America* (New Haven: Yale University Press, 1965), pp. 2–3. Also see M. G. Cooke, ed., *Black American Novelists: A Collection of Critical Essays* (Englewood Cliffs, N.J.: Prentice-Hall, 1971), p. 3.

7.   "Reflections on Richard Wright: A Symposium on an Exiled Native Son," in *Anger, and Beyond: The Negro Writer in the United States*, ed. Herbert Hill (New York: Harper and Row, 1966), p. 207; Edward Margolies, *Native Sons: A Critical Study of Twentieth-Century Negro American Authors* (Philadelphia: J. B. Lippincott Co., 1968), p. 67.

8.   *The Writer in the South: Studies in a Literary Community* (Athens: University of Georgia Press, 1972), p. xiv.

9.   Saunders Redding, "The Negro Writer and American Literature," in *Anger, and Beyond*, pp. 3–4.

10. Bone, *Negro Novel*, p. 46.

11. Margolies, *Native Sons*, p. 40. Also see Frank Durham, "Jean Toomer's Vision of the Southern Negro," *Southern Historical Review* 6 (1972): 13–22.

12. Bradbury, *Renaissance*, pp. 3–4. Some of these difficulties are discussed in Joseph F. Trimmer's *Black American Literature: Notes on the Problem of Definition* (Muncie, Ind.: Ball State University Press, 1971).

13. For a full discussion of Twain as a southern author, see Louis D. Rubin, Jr., "Mark Twain and the Postwar Scene," *The Writer in the South*, (Athens: University of Georgia Press, 1972), pp. 34–81.

14. Hoffman, *The Art of Southern Fiction;* C. Hugh Holman, *Three Modes of Modern Southern Fiction: Ellen Glasgow, William Faulkner, Thomas Wolfe* (Athens: University of Georgia Press, 1966); and Rubin, *The Writer in the South*.

Chapter II: *Trunk and Branch*

1.   Saunders Redding, "The Negro Writer and American Literature," in *Anger and Beyond*, pp. 3–4. Also see Julian D. Mason, "Charles W. Chesnutt as Southern Author," *Mississippi Quarterly* 20 (1967): 77–89.

2.   Unless otherwise indicated, all biographical data are from *Charles*

Waddell Chesnutt: Pioneer of the Color Line (Chapel Hill: University of North Carolina Press, 1952), by Chesnutt's daughter, Helen M. Chesnutt; and *Charles W. Chesnutt: America's First Great Black Novelist* (Hamden, Conn.: Archon Books, 1974), by J. Noel Heermance.

3. See the 1899 photograph of Chesnutt included as a frontispiece in Helen Chesnutt's biography.

4. "Exactly how those stories, written in the local color tradition and in the same form as Page and (to a lesser degree) Harris used, completely reverse the stereotype and turn the form against itself is in my view the most fascinating thing about Chesnutt's work." Louis D. Rubin, Jr., to me, 17 April 1978.

5. The mulatto, tragic or not, is the subject of much important southern fiction, black and white. Twain's *The Tragedy of Pudd'nhead Wilson*, James Weldon Johnson's *The Autobiography of an Ex-Coloured Man*, Faulkner's *Absalom, Absalom!* and *Light in August* are a few of the more obvious examples. Jean Toomer, like Chesnutt, was such a figure.

6. Quoted by Chesnutt, *Charles Waddell Chesnutt*, p. 147.

7. Ibid., p. 21.

8. See Sylvia Lyons Render, "Tar Heelia in Chesnutt," *College Language Association Journal* 9 (September, 1965):39–50.

9. Julian D. Mason, Jr., believes that *The Colonel's Dream*, "more than any other of Chesnutt's fiction, shows his love and genuine concern for the South and her people" (p. 88). This judgment may well be correct, but the social criticism expressed in this novel seems to have been deliberately softened in response to the harsh criticism elicited by *The Marrow of Tradition*. And it is his only novel (including the unpublished *Quarry*) which does not focus centrally on the problem of the mulatto.

10. Charles Waddell Chesnutt, *The House behind the Cedars* (New York: Macmillan Co., 1969), p. 140. All subsequent references to this work will be noted parenthetically in the text.

11. R. Z. Sheppard, "Home Games," a review of Robert Early's *The Jealous Ear*, in *Time* (30 July 1973):69.

12. A booklet entitled "Virginia," published in 1976 by the Virginia State Travel Service, includes a picture of a young man on horseback as he tries to pierce an iron ring. The accompanying copy reads, "For more than 150 years, dashing Virginian knights have been competing in the Natural Chimneys Jousting Tournament, racing down the course under the eyes of their 'Queen of Love and Beauty.'"

13. Chesnutt calls his fictional Wilmington, "Wellington." Charles Waddell

Chesnutt, *The Marrow of Tradition* (Ann Arbor: University of Michigan Press, 1969). All references to this work will be noted parenthetically in the text.

14. Ibid., pp. xiii–xiv.

Chapter III: *Themes and Cadences*

1. Unless otherwise indicated, all biographical data are from *Along This Way: The Autobiography of James Weldon Johnson* (New York: Viking Press, 1933) and Eugene Levy's *James Weldon Johnson: Black Leader, Black Voice* (Chicago: University of Chicago Press, 1973).

2. "Johnson is the only true artist among the early Negro novelists. His superior craftsmanship is undoubtedly due to his early training in the musical comedy field." Bone, *Negro Novel*, p. 46.

3. See James Weldon Johnson, *God's Trombones* (New York: Viking Press, 1927), p. 7.

4. In his excellent biography, Eugene Levy discusses both Johnson's sources for *The Autobiography of an Ex-Coloured Man* and its relationship as a fictional confession to the narratives of such black autobiographers as Booker T. Washington and Frederick Douglass. He also argues that the "octoroon theme" is of relatively minor importance in black fiction (pp. 130–31). It seems to me that this argument is misleading on two grounds. First of all, however unimportant they seem now, a substantial number of the novels written by black writers between emancipation and Richard Wright's time were about blacks who appeared to be Caucasian. Secondly, although such fictional figures are no longer common, the central issue of almost all black American fiction, both before and after Richard Wright, is the black man's identity. The primary function of the mulatto figure was, of course, to dramatize the problem of the black man's ambiguous identity.

5. James Weldon Johnson, *The Autobiography of an Ex-Coloured Man* (New York: Hill and Wang, 1960), p. 3. All subsequent references to this work will be indicated parenthetically in the text.

6. Eugene Levy cites Faulkner's *Light in August* as a novel in which the octoroon appears as a major character (p. 131). As Cleanth Brooks clearly demonstrates in his introduction to the novel, neither Joe Christmas nor anyone else in or out of *Light in August* has any specific information about the racial makeup of Joe's father. "Faulkner could hardly have stressed more emphatically that Joe's status as a 'nigger' is a state of mind rather than a consequence of his possessing some Negro genes, nor could he have shown more persuasively that for Joe the no-

tion that he is a Negro is part of his general alienation from the community." *Light in August* (New York: Random House, Modern Library, 1968), p. vii. In 1912, when Johnson was writing, the point may well have been, as Levy says, that the usefulness of the mulatto lay "largely in the fact that the octoroon is 'like' a white man yet is not one." But the larger significance of this figure as used throughout southern fiction, black and white, is that he is an emblem for all men who are either without identity, or whose identity is imposed from the outside on the basis of appearances, rather than from the inside based on what they are.

7. Although he did not write before the Civil War and certainly did not accept the white southern attitude toward race, Charles Waddell Chesnutt among black southern novelists is more nearly a southern man of letters than he is an imaginative author.

8. Of course, it is equally true that the white southern writer who is outside the black culture also does not participate fully in all aspects of southern life.

9. Both here (p. 87) and in his original preface to *The Book of American Negro Poetry* (New York: Harcourt, Brace and Co., 1922, 1958), pp. 10–11, Johnson argues that the Uncle Remus stories, the Jubilee songs (especially as performed by the Fisk Jubilee Singers), ragtime music, and the cake walk demonstrate the originality and artistic ability of the Negro race.

Chapter IV: *Song of the South*

1. Unless otherwise specified, all biographical data are from Turner's "Jean Toomer: Exile," in *In a Minor Chord: Three Afro-American Writers and Their Search for Identity* (Carbondale: Southern Illinois University Press, 1971). Based to a large degree upon the letters and various unpublished manuscripts (including four autobiographical pieces written between 1929 and 1947) held in the Jean Toomer collection at Fisk University, Professor Turner's splendid essay is indispensable to any serious Toomer student.

2. Quoted by Arna Bontemps, *Cane* (New York: Harper and Row, 1969), pp. viii–ix.

3. Quoted by Turner, "Jean Toomer," p. 34.

4. Ibid., pp. 14, 124–25.

5. *Three Stories and Ten Poems* (1923) and *In Our Time* (1925) were written contemporaneously with *Cane*. Bone, *Negro Novel*, describes part one of *Cane* as "a kind of Southern *Winesburg, Ohio*," p. 82.

6. Among others, William Van O'Connor in *The Tangled Fire of William Faulkner* and Harry Runyun in *A Faulkner Glossary* take the opposite position.
7. Richard S. Kennedy, "Thomas Wolfe's Fiction: The Question of Genre," in *Thomas Wolfe and the Glass of Time*, ed. Paschal Reeves (Athens: University of Georgia Press, 1971), pp. 28–29.
8. *Cane*, p. 1. Subsequent references are cited parenthetically in the text.
9. William Faulkner, *The Hamlet* (New York: Random House, Modern Library, 1931), p. 165.
10. Thomas Wolfe, *Look Homeward, Angel* (New York: Charles Scribner's Sons, 1952), pp. 137, 139, 229. Subsequent references will be cited parenthetically in the text.

Chapter V: *A Clear Case*

1. "Reflections on Richard Wright," p. 207.
2. Margolies, *Native Sons*, p. 67.
3. The primary source for the biographical data in this essay is the encyclopedic *The Unfinished Quest of Richard Wright*, by Michel Fabre (New York: William Morrow and Co., 1973). In addition, I have found *Richard Wright*, by David Bakish (New York: Ungar, 1973), *Richard Wright*, by Milton and Patricia Rickels (Austin, Tex.: Steck-Vaughn, 1970), and *Richard Wright: A Biography*, by Constance Webb (New York: Putnam, 1968) most helpful.
4. Richard Crossman, ed. (New York: Harper and Row, 1950).
5. Richard Wright, *Black Boy: A Record of Childhood and Youth* (New York: Harper and Row, 1966), p. 284. All subsequent references to this work will be noted parenthetically in the text.
6. "Reflections on Richard Wright," p. 201.
7. "Richard Wright's Blues," in *Shadow and Act* (New York: Random House, Vintage Press, 1972), p. 78.
8. I have found no specific indication in any of the major studies that Wright had read Thomas Wolfe. Certainly Wolfe is not listed with Dreiser, Mencken, Sinclair Lewis, Gertrude Stein, Dostoyevsky, and Kafka as one of the major literary influences on Wright. Interestingly enough, Edward Aswell, Wolfe's editor at Harper and Row, was also Wright's close friend and editor. And Paul Green, who collaborated with Wright in adapting *Native Son* for the stage production directed by Orson Welles and John Houseman, was a freshman at the University of North Carolina with Wolfe. Green and Wolfe both studied playwriting with Frederic H. Koch and wrote plays produced by Koch's Car-

olina Playmakers. One who knew him in the mid-1930s remembers seeing some of Wright's manuscripts at the time: "All I remember about them is an impression of a tremendous flow of words, like Thomas Wolfe, quite undisciplined, impelled by an obvious urge to communicate a deep sense of wrong." Fabre, *Unfinished Quest*, p. 109.

9. *Look Homeward, Angel*, p. 3.
10. *The Web and the Rock* (New York: Harper and Row, 1939), pp. 30–31.
11. "The South and the Faraway Country," pp. 10–11.
12. *Of Time and the River* (New York: Charles Scribner's Sons, 1935), pp. 91–92.
13. *You Can't Go Home Again* (New York: Harper and Row, 1940), p. 327.
14. Fabre, *Unfinished Quest*, pp. 111, 332.
15. Ibid., p. 601.
16. Joseph Blotner, *Faulkner: A Biography* (New York: Random House, 1974), 2:1190–91; Webb, *Richard Wright*, pp. 208–9.
17. Fabre, *Unfinished Quest*, pp. 354–55.
18. In "Richard Wright in a Moment of Truth," *The Southern Literary Journal* 3, no. 2 (Spring, 1971):3–17, Blyden Jackson explores "Big Boy Leaves Home," one of the stories that make up *Uncle Tom's Children*, as a means of seeing that Wright was "a Mississippian, a Southerner, and to call him that is not merely to demand due recognition for the statistics of his birth and residence during his plastic years, but also to recognize a fact of the utmost importance in understanding the growth and peculiarities of his artistic imagination."
19. *Native Son* (New York: Harper and Row, 1966), p. 288. This edition also includes Wright's introductory essay, "How Bigger Was Born."
20. *Light in August* (New York: Random House, Modern Library, 1968), p. 439.
21. There are other "Christ figures" in *Native Son*. When Jan tries to accept his share of the guilt for what happened to Bigger, "the word had become flesh" (p. 268). When Mr. Dalton is asked at the inquest if he has any responsibility for Bigger's inability to have a meaningful life, he asks, "Do you want me to die and atone for a suffering I never caused? I'm not responsible for the state of this world" (p. 274).

Chapter VI: *The Shadow of the Past*

1. All biographical information is from Ellison's statements in *Shadow and Act* (New York: Random House, Vintage Press, 1972), and from "Indivisible Man" by Ralph Ellison and James Allan McFerguson, *The Atlantic* 226, no. 6 (December, 1970): 45–60.

2. Noel Schraufnagel, *From Apology to Protest: The Black American Novel* (Deland, Fla.: Everett/Edwards, 1973), p. 87.
3. *Shadow and Act*, pp. 5–8.
4. Holman, *Three Modes of Modern Southern Fiction*, pp. 51, 53.
5. Louis D. Rubin, Jr., "'The Begum of Bengal': Mark Twain and the South," in *William Elliott Shoots a Bear: Essays on the Southern Literary Imagination* (Baton Rouge: Louisiana State University Press, 1975), pp. 30–31.
6. "Indivisible Man," pp. 53, 59. On a more personal level, Willie Morris describes his early impressions of Ellison: "I recognized from the first his distinctive *Southernness*, and how similar his was to my own. . . . We shared the same easygoing conversation; the casual talk and the telling of stories, in the Southern verbal jam-session way; the sense of family and the past and people out of the past; the congenial social manner and the mischievous laughter; the fondness of especial *detail* and the suspicion of the more grandiose generalizations about human existence; the love of the American language in its accuracy and vividness and simplicity; the obsession with the sensual experience of America in all its extravagance and diversity; the love of animals and sports, of the outdoors and sour mash; the distrust in the face of provocation of certain manifestations of Eastern intellectualism, particularly in its more academic and sociological forms." *North toward Home* (Boston: Houghton Mifflin Co., 1967), pp. 384–85.
7. C. Hugh Holman, *The Immoderate Past: The Southern Writer and History* (Athens: University of Georgia Press, 1977), p. 1.
8. Ibid., p. 93.
9. Ibid., p. 68.
10. *Invisible Man* (New York: Vintage, 1972). Subsequent references will be cited parenthetically within the text.
11. Ellis Burden's mother was Cass Mastern's sister. But since Jack Burden is not Ellis Burden's son, Cass is not his blood relative. Cass is, of course, one of Jack's spiritual fathers, his life an embodiment of the web theory that Jack comes to accept.
12. Booker T. Washington, *Up From Slavery*, in *The Booker T. Washington Papers*, vol. 1, *The Autobiographical Writings*, ed. Louis R. Harlan (Urbana: University of Illinois Press, 1972), pp. 330–34.
13. "Indivisible Man," pp. 47–48.

Chapter VII: *Products of the Southern Condition*

1. Holman, *The Immoderate Past*, p. 35.

Index

Agrarianism, 14, 45, 46, 49, 52, 82
Alger, Horatio, 10, 86, 89, 90, 91
American Naturalists, 79
Anderson, Sherwood, 42; *Winesburg, Ohio*, 43
Armstrong, Louis, 85
Atlantic Monthly, 10, 11, 55
Attaway, William, 7, 84; *Blood on the Forge*, 84
Autobiography: in *Cane*, 43; in *Black Boy*, 55, 56, 57, 62, 100; in *Shadow and Act*, 81

Baker, Houston A., Jr., 5, 100
Baldwin, James, 3
Bible: in *House behind the Cedars*, 14; in *God's Trombones*, 27; in *Invisible Man*, 91, 94
Black myth: in *Invisible Man*, 86, 87, 88, 89, 90, 92, 93
Black nationalism: in *Invisible Man*, 95

Black-white relationship. *See* Racial relationship
Bledsoe, Mr. (in *Invisible Man*), 50, 89, 90, 91, 92, 95, 96
Blues: in *Invisible Man*, 85, 88, 91
Bon, Charles (in *Absalom, Absalom!*), 23, 28, 29, 33, 74, 75
Bone, Robert A., 5, 20, 42, 43; *The Negro Novel in America*, 20
Bontemps, Arna, 6, 7, 54, 99; "Reflections on Richard Wright," 54; "The Negro Renaissance: Jean Toomer and the Harlem Writers of the 1920's," 99
Bradbury, John M., 4, 7, 101
Brooks, Cleanth, 29, 42, 77
Burden, Jack (in *All the King's Men*), 20, 22, 24, 30, 34, 43, 50, 85, 88 91, 92, 95, 96, 97

Cabell, James Branch, 6, 100
Cable, George W., 11, 27

Capote, Truman, 13, 46, 52, 72, 73, 79, 100; *Other Voices, Other Rooms*, 46, 72

Carteret, Major (in *The Marrow of Tradition*), 19, 20, 21

Carteret, Olivia Merkell (in *The Marrow of Tradition*), 19, 20, 21, 23

Chesnutt, Charles, 6, 7, 9–25, 27, 31, 32, 70, 71, 79, 84, 86, 99; early life, 9, 10; biography of Frederick Douglass, 10; *The Conjure Woman*, 10, 11; "Goophered Grapevine," 10, 11; published in *Atlantic Monthly*, 10; *The Wife of His Youth and Other Stories of the Color Line*, 10; *The Colonel's Dream*, 11; critical reception, 11; *The House behind the Cedars*, 11, 12–19, 21, 22, 24, 27, 29; *The Quarry*, 11; receives Spingarn Medal, 11; compared with Faulkner, 12, 14, 21, 22, 23, 24; compared with Wolfe, 12; compared with O'Connor, 14; compared with Dickens, 16, 20; compared with Scott, 16, 17; compared with Warren, 24; compared with Johnson, 27; compared with Toomer, 39

Christmas, Joe (in *Light in August*), 5, 29, 32, 50, 73, 74, 75, 76, 77, 78, 79

Clemens, Samuel. *See* Twain, Mark

Collins, Carvel, 42

Compson, Quentin (in *Absalom, Absalom!*), 28, 33, 49, 69, 96, 97

Conjure stories, 10, 12, 27

Cummings, E. E., 42; *Eimi*, 42

The Daily American, 26

The Daily Worker, 55

Davidson, Donald, 46

Defoe, Daniel, 33, 41

Dialect, 10, 27

Dickens, Charles, 16, 20

Dos Passos, John, 42, 43; *U.S.A.*, 42, 43

Dostoevsky, Feodor, 3

Douglass, Frederick, 96

Dreiser, Theodore, 79

Eliot, T. S., 87

Ellington, Duke, 85

Ellison, Ralph, 3, 5, 6, 7, 8, 52, 55, 80–98, 100; "The World and the Jug," 3; on Richard Wright, 3; *Invisible Man*, 4, 28, 31, 55, 80, 83, 84–98, 100; early life, 80; compared with Faulkner, 80, 84, 94, 96–97, 98; *Shadow and Act*, 80, 81; wins National Book Award, 81; self-description, 82–83; compared with Twain, 82; compared with Warren, 84, 88, 94, 97, 98; compared with Glasgow, 98; compared with James, 98; compared with Styron, 98

Family, importance of, 6, 21, 96; in *A Marrow of Tradition*, 21; in *Black Boy*, 64, 65; in *Invisible Man*, 96

Farnsworth, Robert N., 21, 23

Fathers, Sam (in *Go Down, Moses*), 12, 96

Faulkner, William, 3, 4, 5, 6, 12, 13, 20–36 passim, 46, 49, 51, 52, 69–79 passim, 84, 88, 94, 98, 100, 101; *Light in August*, 20, 29,

74, 76, 77, 90; *Absalom, Absalom!*, 21, 28, 29, 33, 80, 86, 94, 97; *The Sound and the Fury*, 27, 70, 80, 94, 97; *Go Down, Moses*, 42, 96; *The Unvanquished*, 42; *The Hamlet*, 45, 51, 73; "A Rose for Emily," 46, 86; *A Fable*, 71; *Sanctuary*, 88; *Sartoris/Flags in the Dust*, 88
Federal Negro Theatre, 55
Federal Writers Project, 80
Fertility figures. *See* Pagan inheritance
Fictional thesaurus, 42
Fielding, Henry, 41; *Joseph Andrews*, 13
Finn, Huck (in *The Adventures of Huckleberry Finn*), 13, 43, 81
Folklore, 6, 10, 12, 100; in *God's Trombones*, 27; in *The Autobiography of an Ex-Coloured Man*, 34, 35, 100; in *Invisible Man*, 83, 98
Forster, E. M., 5, 8
Frank, Waldo, 39, 40, 41; *City Block*, 42
Free will vs. determinism, 99, 100; in *The House behind the Cedars*, 24; in *Native Son*, 71, 77, 78, 79, 100

Gaines, Ernest, 7, 84; *The Autobiography of Miss Jane Pittman*, 84
Gant, Eugene (in *Look Homeward, Angel*), 13, 14, 30, 43, 44, 45, 47, 49, 62, 63, 64, 65, 66, 67
Garvey, Marcus, 93, 95
Glasgow, Ellen, 6, 84, 98, 100
God: in *Cane*, 45; in *Invisible Man*, 85, 90
Gothic, elements of, 46, 52; in

"Box Seat," 47; in "Kabnis," 49; in *Native Son*, 71, 72, 73, 79, 100
Grove, Lena (in *Light in August*), 22, 44, 77, 78
Gurdjieff, Georges Ivanovitch, 41

Haley, Alex, 95; *Roots*, 95
Hardy, Thomas, 20
Harris, Joel Chandler, 10, 27
Hegel, Georg Wilhelm Friedrich, 84, 98
Hemingway, Ernest, 3, 42
Henderson, George Wylie, 7
History, relationship between man and. *See* Past, importance of
Hoffman, Frederick J., 4, 5, 8, 101
Holman, C. Hugh, 8, 21, 82, 83, 84, 98; *The Immoderate Past: The Southern Writer and History*, 21
Howe, Irving, 3; "Black Boys and Native Sons," 3
Howells, William Dean, 11
Hurston, Zora Neale, 7
Huxley, Aldous, 42; *Ape and Essence*, 42

Identity, individual's search for, 6, 13–14, 43, 52, 60, 71; in *The House behind the Cedars*, 13, 14, 15, 16, 17, 18, 19; in *The Autobiography of an Ex-Coloured Man*, 28, 29; in *Cane*, 44; in *Black Boy*, 60; in *Native Son*, 71, 73, 74, 79. *See also* Identity, racial
Identity, racial: in "Bona and Paul," 48, 49; in *Invisible Man*, 83; in *The Autobiography of an Ex-Coloured Man*, 100. *See also* Identity, individual's search for

Illinois Writers Project, 55
Innocence, individual's loss of,
   13–14; in *The House behind the
   Cedars*, 13–14. *See also* Identity,
   individual's search for
Inverted Christ figure: in *Native
   Son*, 71, 76, 79, 100, 109 (n. 21)
Invisible man metaphor: in "The
   Man Who Lived Underground,"
   55; in *Invisible Man*, 84, 85
Isolation, 52, 60; in "Avey," 47; in
   "Theater," 47; in "Kabnis," 49; in
   Black Boy, 60; in *Native Son*,
   74, 76

Jack, Brother (in *Invisible Man*),
   93, 95
James, Henry, 11, 84, 98
Johnson, James Weldon, 6, 7, 11,
   26–37, 41, 51, 52, 70, 71, 79, 84,
   86, 100; early life, 26; *Along This
   Way*, 26, 27; *The Book of American Negro Poetry*, 26, 41; *The
   Book of American Negro Spirituals*, 26, 35; *God's Trombones*,
   26, 27, 35, 36, 51; *The Autobiography of an Ex-Coloured
   Man*, 27–37, 51, 85, 100; compared with Chesnutt, 27, 29, 31,
   32, 37; receives honors, 27; receives Spingarn Medal, 27; compared with Ellison, 28, 31, 85;
   compared with Faulkner, 28, 29,
   31, 32, 33, 34; compared with
   Mann, 31; compared with Twain,
   31, 32; compared with Wolfe, 31;
   compared with Defoe, 33; compared with O'Connor, 34; compared with Styron, 34; compared
   with Warren, 34
Joyce, James, 42, 43, 57; *Ulysses*,

42, 43, 70; *A Portrait of the Artist as a Young Man*, 57

Kabnis (in "Kabnis"), 49–51
Kafka, Franz, 45, 73
Keats, John, 85
Kennedy, Richard S., 42
Knox, Joel (in *Other Voices, Other
   Rooms*), 13, 46, 72
Ku Klux Klan, 22, 81, 82

Lanier, Sidney, 38
Locus, sense of, 6
Lyricism. *See* Oral tradition
Lytton, Edward Bulwer, 20, 29;
   The Last of the Barons, 30

McCaslin, Ike (in *Go Down,
   Moses*), 13, 24, 34, 96
McCullers, Carson, 4, 6, 14, 20,
   31, 32, 47, 52, 71, 73, 79, 100;
   The Heart Is a Lonely Hunter,
   32, 71
Malraux, André, 3
Mann, Thomas, 31
Margolies, Edward, 6, 54
Marxism: in *Native Son*, 78, 79; in
   Invisible Man, 93, 94, 98
Mastern, Cass (in *All the King's
   Men*), 24, 86
Maupassant, Guy De, 11
Meriwether, James B., 42
Millgate, Michael, 42
Mulattoes, 11, 27, 105 (n. 5), 106 (n.
   4), 107 (n. 6); in *The House be-
   hind the Cedars*, 18; in *The
   Marrow of Tradition*, 19; in *The
   Autobiography of an Ex-Col-
   oured Man*, 27, 100
Music: in *The Autobiography of an*

Ex-Coloured Man, 28, 30, 33. *See also* Blues

NAACP, 11, 26, 27, 31, 55
Negro Quarterly, 80
New Masses, 80
The New Republic, 71, 80
Nietzsche, Friedrich, 84
Norton, Mr. (in *Invisible Man*), 89, 90, 91, 95

O'Connor, Flannery, 6, 14, 34, 47, 48, 52, 71, 73, 76, 79, 100; *A Late Encounter with the Enemy,* 86
Oral tradition, 6, 27, 51, 52, 94, 100; in *God's Trombones,* 27; in *Cane,* 49; in *The Autobiography of an Ex-Coloured Man,* 51, 100; in *Invisible Man,* 83, 94

Pagan inheritance, 52; in *Cane,* 44, 45, 100
Page, Thomas Nelson, 52
Page, Walter Hines, 11
Past, importance of, 6, 21, 85; in *The House behind the Cedars,* 18, 21, 22; in *The Marrow of Tradition,* 21, 22; in *The Autobiography of an Ex-Coloured Man,* 30, 31; in "Kabnis," 50; in *Invisible Man,* 83, 84, 86, 92, 93, 94, 96, 98, 100
Piedmont society, 82
Poe, Edgar Allen, 52, 73
Protestantism, 6, 34, 36, 98

Racial caste, 31; in *The House behind the Cedars,* 12, 14, 15, 24; in *The Autobiography of an Ex-*
Coloured Man, 28; in *Native Son,* 75
Racial relationship, 6, 100; in *The Marrow of Tradition,* 12; in *The Autobiography of an Ex-Coloured Man,* 34, 35, 37; in *Native Son,* 79, 100
Ransom, John Crowe, 46
Rape: in *Native Son,* 72, 75
Redding, Saunders, 6, 9, 25, 26, 54, 56, "The Negro Writer and American Literature," 9; "James Weldon Johnson (1871–1938)," 26; "Reflections on Richard Wright," 54
Reed, Ishmael, 7
Remus. *See* Uncle Remus
Renaissance, southern black literary, 4, 101
Renascence, southern literary, 6, 101
Rhobert (in *Cane*), 45, 46, 47, 50
Richardson, Samuel, 41
Rubin, Louis D., Jr., 5, 6, 8, 31, 67, 82; *Bibliographical Guide to the Study of Southern Literature,* 82

Scott, Walter, 16, 17, 20, 21, 29, 84; *Ivanhoe,* 16, 17, 21, 30, 96
Simms, William Gilmore, 21, 52, 84, 98, 100
Snopes, Mink (in *The Hamlet*), 24, 73
Southern writers, 4, 5, 24, 25, 101; defined, 7–8; elements common to, 6, 13, 14, 34, 43, 52, 53, 71, 79, 83, 88, 99–100; categories of, 31, 84; relationship to family, 67, 101; relationship to past, 82, 84
Spingarn Medal, 11, 27, 55

Spiritual identity. *See* Identity, in-
dividual's loss of
Stark, Willie (in *All the King's
Men*), 14, 24, 34, 94
Stein, Gertrude, 42
Stowe, Harriet Beecher, 30; *Uncle
Tom's Cabin*, 30
Styron, William, 6, 14, 20, 21, 31,
32, 34, 74, 82, 86, 88, 92, 98,
100; *The Confessions of Nat
Turner*, 32, 74; *Lie Down in
Darkness*, 86, 88
Subterranean withdrawal meta-
phor. *See* Invisible man
metaphor
Sutpen, Thomas (in *Absalom, Ab-
salom!*), 13, 14, 21, 23, 29

Tate, Allen, 46
Thomas, Bigger (in *Native Son*), 5,
32, 71, 72, 73, 74, 75, 76, 77
Toomer, Jean, 5, 6, 7, 8, 38–54,
70, 71, 79, 100; *Cane*, 8, 38,
40–45, 52; early life, 38, 39;
compared with Chesnutt, 39;
compared with Johnson, 39; *A
Fiction and Some Facts*, 41; influenced by Gurdjieff, 41; compared with Wolfe, 43, 44, 45, 47,
49; compared with Faulkner, 44,
49, 50; "Avey," 47; "Box Seat,"
47, 48; compared with Mc-
Cullers, 47; compared with
O'Connor, 47, 48; "Theater," 47;
"Bona and Paul," 48; "Kabnis,"
49–51; compared with Ellison,
50; compared with Warren, 50
Tourgénief, Ivan, 11
Trueblood (in *Invisible Man*), 88,
89, 92
Tryon, George (in *The House be-

hind the Cedars*), 13, 16, 18, 19
Turner, Darwin, 38, 41, 42, 43
Turner, Nat (in *The Confessions of
Nat Turner*), 14, 34, 43
Turpin, Edward Waters, 7
Twain, Mark (Samuel Clemens), 6,
8, 13, 27, 31, 52, 71, 82, 96; *The
Adventures of Huckleberry Finn*,
8, 27

Uncle Remus, 10, 11

Waggoner, Hyatt H., 42
Walden, John (in *The House behind the Cedars*), 12, 13, 14, 15,
16, 17, 18, 22, 29, 74
Walden, Rena (in *The House be-
hind the Cedars*), 12, 13, 15, 16,
17, 18, 22
Walker, Margaret, 7, 84; *Jubilee*,
84
Waller, Fats, 85
Warren, Robert Penn, 6, 14, 19,
20, 21, 30, 32, 34, 46, 51, 52, 73,
82, 84, 85, 86, 94, 98, 100; *All
the King's Men*, 20, 30, 81, 85,
86, 94, 97
Washington, Booker T., 36, 74, 86,
87, 90, 91, 92, 98
Wasteland metaphor: in *Invisible
Man*, 87, 88, 89
Webber, George (in *You Can't Go
Home Again*), 14, 49, 70
Welty, Eudora, 4, 6
White southern myth, 86, 88, 89
Witchcraft. *See* Pagan inheritance
Wolfe, Thomas, 6, 12, 13, 21, 31,
36, 42, 43, 44, 45, 47, 51, 52,
57–70, 68, 100; *Of Time and the
River*, 42, 43, 68, 69; *Look
Homeward, Angel*, 44, 57–70,

79, 100; "Story of the Buried Life," 66

WPA, 55

Wright, Richard, 3, 5, 6, 7, 54–79, 84, 100; *Black Boy*, 4, 55, 56–70, 71, 79, 100; early life, 54–55; awarded Guggenheim Fellowship, 55; awarded Spingarn Medal, 55; "The God That Failed," 55; "I Tried to be a Communist," 55; "The Man Who Lived Underground," 55, 85; influenced by Sartre and Camus, 56; *The Long Dream*, 56, 71; *Native Son*, 56, 70–79, 100; *The Outsider*, 56, 71; *Savage Holiday*, 56; compared with Joyce, 57; with Wolfe, 57–70, 79; on Faulkner, 70–71; compared with Chesnutt, 71, 74, 79; compared with Faulkner, 71, 72, 73, 74, 75, 76, 77, 79; compared with Johnson, 71, 79; compared with Toomer, 71, 79; Faulkner on, 71; reviews *The Heart Is a Lonely Hunter*, 71; compared with Capote, 72, 73, 79; compared with Steinbeck, 72; compared with McCullers, 73, 79; compared with O'Connor, 73, 79; compared with Styron, 74